How to Form Your Own Corporation

HOW TO FORM YOUR OWN CORPORATION

with forms

Third Edition

W. Kelsea Eckert
Arthur G. Sartorius, III
Mark Warda
Attorneys at Law

Sphinx® Publishing
A Division of Sourcebooks
Naperville, IL

Third Edition, 2001

Published by: **Sphinx® Publishing, a division of Sourcebooks, Inc.®**

Naperville Office
P.O. Box 4410
Naperville, Illinois 60567-4410
(630) 961-3900
FAX: 630-961-2168

This publication is designed to provide accurate and authoritative information in regard to the subject matter covered. It is sold with the understanding that the publisher is not engaged in rendering legal, accounting, or other professional service. If legal advice or other expert assistance is required, the services of a competent professional person should be sought.
From a Declaration of Principles Jointly Adopted by a Committee of the
American Bar Association and a Committee of Publishers and Associations

This product is not a substitute for legal advice.

Disclaimer required by Texas statutes.

Library of Congress Cataloging-in-Publication Data
Eckert, W. Kelsea.
   How to form your own corporation: with forms / W. Kelsea Eckert, Arthur G.
Sartorius, III, Mark Warda.—3rd ed.
      p. cm.—(Self-help law kit wih forms)
   Includes index.
   ISBN 1-57248-133-1 (alk. paper)
   1. Corporation law—United States—Popular works. 2. Corporation law—United States—
Forms. I. Sartorius, Arthur G. II. Warda, Mark. III. Title. IV. Series.

KF1414.6.E29 2000
346.73'066–dc21
                                                                                    00-053190
                                                                                    CIP

Printed and bound in the United States of America.

HS Paperback — 10 9 8 7 6 5 4 3 2 1

CONTENTS

Using Self-Help Law Books

Before using a self-help law book, you should realize the advantages and disadvantages of doing your own legal work and understand the challenges and diligence that this requires.

THE GROWING
TREND

Rest assured that you won't be the first or only person handling your own legal matter. For example, in some states, more than seventy-five percent of the people in divorces and other cases represent themselves. Because of the high cost of legal services, this is a major trend and many courts are struggling to make it easier for people to represent themselves. However, some courts are not happy with people who do not use attorneys and refuse to help them in any way. For some, the attitude is, "Go to the law library and figure it out for yourself."

We write and publish self-help law books to give people an alternative to the often complicated and confusing legal books found in most law libraries. We have made the explanations of the law as simple and easy to understand as possible. Of course, unlike an attorney advising an individual client, we cannot cover every conceivable possibility.

COST/VALUE
ANALYSIS

Whenever you shop for a product or service, you are faced with various levels of quality and price. In deciding what product or service to buy, you make a cost/value analysis on the basis of your willingness to pay and the quality you desire.

When buying a car, you decide whether you want transportation, comfort, status, or sex appeal. Accordingly, you decide among such choices as a Neon, a Lincoln, a Rolls Royce, or a Porsche. Before making a decision, you usually weigh the merits of each option against the cost.

When you get a headache, you can take a pain reliever (such as aspirin) or visit a medical specialist for a neurological examination. Given this choice, most people, of course, take a pain reliever, since it costs only pennies; whereas a medical examination costs hundreds of dollars and takes a lot of time. This is usually a logical choice because it is rare to need anything more than a pain reliever for a headache. But in some cases, a headache may indicate a brain tumor and failing to see a specialist right away can result in complications. Should everyone with a headache go to a specialist? Of course not, but people treating their own illnesses must realize that they are betting on the basis of their cost/value analysis of the situation. They are taking the most logical option.

The same cost/value analysis must be made when deciding to do one's own legal work. Many legal situations are very straight forward, requiring a simple form and no complicated analysis. Anyone with a little intelligence and a book of instructions can handle the matter without outside help.

But there is always the chance that complications are involved that only an attorney would notice. To simplify the law into a book like this, several legal cases often must be condensed into a single sentence or paragraph. Otherwise, the book would be several hundred pages long and too complicated for most people. However, this simplification necessarily leaves out many details and nuances that would apply to special or unusual situations. Also, there are many ways to interpret most legal questions. Your case may come before a judge who disagrees with the analysis of our authors.

Therefore, in deciding to use a self-help law book and to do your own legal work, you must realize that you are making a cost/value analysis. You have decided that the money you will save in doing it yourself outweighs the chance that your case will not turn out to your satisfaction. Most people handling their own simple legal matters never have a problem, but occasionally people find that it ended up costing them more to have an attorney straighten out the situation than it would have if they had hired an attorney in the beginning. Keep this in mind while handling your case, and be sure to consult an attorney if you feel you might need further guidance.

LOCAL RULES   The next thing to remember is that a book which covers the law for the entire nation, or even for an entire state, cannot possibly include every procedural difference of every jurisdiction. Whenever possible, we provide the exact form needed; however, in some areas, each county, or even each judge, may require unique forms and procedures. In our state books, our forms usually cover the majority of counties in the state, or provide examples of the type of form which will be required. In our national books, our forms are sometimes even more general in nature but are designed to give a good idea of the type of form that will be needed in most locations. Nonetheless, keep in mind that your state, county, or judge may have a requirement, or use a form, that is not included in this book.

CHANGES IN   You should not necessarily expect to be able to get all of the informa-
THE LAW   tion and resources you need solely from within the pages of this book. This book will serve as your guide, giving you specific information whenever possible and helping you to find out what else you will need to know. This is just like if you decided to build your own backyard deck. You might purchase a book on how to build decks. However, such a book would not include the building codes and permit requirements of every city, town, county, and township in the nation; nor would it include the lumber, nails, saws, hammers, and other materials and tools you would need to actually build the deck. You would use the book as your guide, and then do some work and research involving such matters as whether you need a permit of some kind, what type and grade of wood are available in your area, whether to use hand tools or power tools, and how to use those tools.

Before using the forms in a book like this, you should check with your court clerk to see if there are any local rules of which you should be aware, or local forms you will need to use. Often, such forms will require the same information as the forms in the book but are merely laid out differently or use slightly different language. They will sometimes require additional information.

Besides being subject to local rules and practices, the law is subject to change at any time. The courts and the legislatures of all fifty states are constantly revising the laws. It is possible that while you are reading this book, some aspect of the law is being changed.

In most cases, the change will be of minimal significance. A form will be redesigned, additional information will be required, or a waiting period will be extended. As a result, you might need to revise a form, file an extra form, or wait out a longer time period; these types of changes will not usually affect the outcome of your case. On the other hand, sometimes a major part of the law is changed, the entire law in a particular area is rewritten, or a case that was the basis of a central legal point is overruled. In such instances, your entire ability to pursue your case may be impaired.

Again, you should weigh the value of your case against the cost of an attorney and make a decision as to what you believe is in your best interest.

INTRODUCTION

Each year hundreds of thousands of corporations are registered in this country and it is not a coincidence that the largest businesses in the world are corporations. The corporation is the preferred method of doing business for most people because it offers many advantages over partnerships and sole proprietorships.

The main reason people incorporate is to avoid personal liability. While sole proprietors and partners have all of their personal assets at risk, corporate shareholders risk only what they paid for their stock. With so many people ready to sue for any reason, or for no reason, the corporation is one of the few inexpensive protections left.

Creating a simple corporation is very easy and it is the purpose of this book to explain, in simple language, how you can do it yourself. A simple corporation, as used in this book, is one in which there are five or fewer shareholders and all of them are active in the business. If you plan to sell stock to someone who is not active in the business, or to have six or more shareholders, you should seek the advice of an attorney. However, some guidance is provided throughout this book as to what some of the concerns will be in these circumstances.

If your situation is in any way complicated or involves factors not mentioned in this book, you should seek the advice of an attorney practicing corporate law. The cost of a short consultation can be a lot cheaper than the consequences of violating the law.

If you plan to sell stock to outside investors you should consult with a lawyer who specializes in securities laws. Selling a few thousand shares of stock to friends and neighbors may sound like an easy way to raise capital for your business, but it is not! After the stock market crash of the 1930s, both the federal government and the states passed laws regulating the sale of securities. There are harsh criminal penalties for violators and the laws don't have many loopholes. The basic rules are explained in Chapter 5.

This book also explains the basics of corporate taxation, but you should consult a tax guide or an accountant before deciding what is best for you. Starting with an efficient system of bookkeeping can save you both time and money.

Good luck with your new business!

WHAT IS A CORPORATION? 1

A corporation is a legal "person" which can be created under state law. As a person, a corporation has certain rights and obligations including the right to do business in its own name and the obligation to pay taxes. Some laws use the words "natural persons." A "natural person" refers only to human beings. A corporation can only be referred to as a "person" under the law, and is never referred to as a "natural person."

Business corporations were invented hundreds of years ago to promote risky ventures such as voyages to explore the new world. Prior to the use of corporations, if a venture failed, persons who invested in it faced the possibility of unlimited liability. By using a corporation, many people were able to invest fixed sums of money for a new venture, and if the venture made money, they shared the profits. If the venture failed, the most they could lose was their initial investment.

The reasons for having a corporation are the same today: corporations allow investors to put up money for new ventures without risk of further liability. While our legal system is making people liable in more and more situations, the corporation remains one of the few shields from liability that has not yet been abandoned.

Before forming a corporation you should be familiar with these common corporate terms which will be used in the text:

ARTICLES OF INCORPORATION

The *Articles of Incorporation* (in some states referred to as the *Charter* or the *Certificate of Incorporation*) is the document that is filed with the appropriate state agency to start the corporation. (In all but twelve states, this agency is the Secretary of State. In these other states it may be called the Department of State, the Division of Corporations, or some similar name. Appendix A will tell you what name is used in your state. For simplicity, the phrase "Secretary of State" will be used to designate this agency.) In most cases, it legally needs to contain only five basic statements. Some corporations have lengthy Articles of Incorporation, but this just makes it harder to make changes in the corporate structure. It is usually better to keep the Articles short and put the details in the bylaws. (See Appendix B for Articles of Incorporation.)

SHAREHOLDER

A *shareholder* is a person who owns stock in a corporation. In most small corporations, the shareholders are the same as the officers and directors, but in large corporations most shareholders are not officers or directors. Sometimes small corporations have shareholders who are not officers, such as when the stock is in one spouse's name and the other spouse runs the business. Specific laws regarding issuance of shares and shareholders' rights vary from state to state and are listed in the various state statutes. Shareholders must meet once a year to elect directors and make other major decisions for the corporation.

BOARD OF DIRECTORS

The *Board of Directors* is the controlling body of a corporation that makes major corporate decisions and elects the officers. It usually meets just once a year. In most states a corporation can have one director (who can also hold all offices and own all the stock). In a small corporation, the board members are usually also officers.

OFFICERS

Officers of a corporation usually include a president, secretary, treasurer, and vice president. These persons typically run the day-to-day affairs of the business. They are elected each year by the Board of Directors. In most states, one person can hold all of the offices of a corporation. (See Appendix A.)

REGISTERED
AGENT

The *Registered Agent* (in some states referred to as the *Resident Agent*) is the person designated by the corporation to receive legal papers which may be served on the corporation. The registered agent should be regularly available at the *registered office* of the corporation. The registered office can be the corporate office, the office of the corporation's attorney, or the office of another person who is the registered agent.

In most states, the person accepting the position as registered agent must sign a statement that he or she understands the duties and responsibilities of the position. These are spelled out in the state statutes listed in Appendix A.

BYLAWS

Bylaws are the rules governing the structure and operation of the corporation. Typically the bylaws will set out rules for the board of directors, officers, and shareholders, and will explain corporate formalities.

SHOULD YOU INCORPORATE? 2

Before forming a corporation, a business owner or prospective business owner should become familiar with the advantages and disadvantages of incorporating.

ADVANTAGES

The following are some of the advantages that a corporation has over other forms of businesses such as sole proprietorships and partnerships.

LIMITED
LIABILITY

The main reason for forming a corporation is to limit the liability of the owners. In a sole proprietorship or partnership, the owners are personally liable for the debts and liabilities of the business, and in many instances, creditors can go after their personal assets to collect business debts. If a corporation is formed and operated properly, the owners can be protected from all such liability.

Examples:

- ☞ If several people are in *partnership* and one of them makes many extravagant purchases in the name of the partnership, the other partners may be held liable for the full amount of all such purchases. The creditors may be able to take the bank accounts, cars, real estate, and other property of any partner to pay the debts of the partnership. If only one partner has money, he may have to pay all of the debts run up by all the other partners. When doing business as a corporation, the corporation may go bankrupt and the shareholders may lose their initial investment, but the creditors cannot touch the personal assets of the owners.

☞ If a person owns a taxi business as a sole proprietor and one of the drivers cause a terrible accident, the owner can be held liable for the full amount of the damages. If the taxi driver was on drugs and killed several people and the damages amount to millions of dollars more than the insurance coverage, the owner may lose everything he owns. On the other hand, if the business is formed as a corporation, only the corporation would be liable, and if there was not enough money, the stockholder(s) still couldn't be touched personally. An example which carried this to the extreme is as follows: there was once a business owner who had hundreds of taxis. He put one or two in each of hundreds of different corporations which he owned. Each corporation only had minimal insurance and when one taxi was involved in an accident, the owner only lost the assets of that corporation.

WARNING!   If a corporate officer or shareholder does something negligent himself, or signs a debt personally, or guarantees a corporate debt, then the corporation will not protect him from the consequences of his own act or from the debt. Corporate officers can be held liable by the IRS for payroll taxes that have not been paid and some states (e.g. New York) hold them liable for unpaid wages.

Also, if a corporation does not follow the proper corporate formalities, it may be ignored by a court and the owner may be held personally liable. The formalities include having separate bank accounts, holding meetings, and keeping minutes. When a court ignores a corporate structure and holds the owners liable, it is called *piercing the corporate veil*.

CONTINUOUS
EXISTENCE

In all states (except Mississippi), a corporation may have a perpetual existence. When a sole proprietor or partner dies, the assets may go to their heirs but the business does not exist any longer. If the heirs of a business owner want to continue the business in their own names, they will be considered a new business, even if they are using the assets of the old business. With a partnership, the death of one partner may result in dissolution of the business.

Examples:

☞ If a person dies owning a sole proprietorship, his or her spouse may want to continue the business. That person may inherit all of the assets, but will have to start a new business. This means getting new licenses and tax numbers, re-registering the name, and establishing credit from scratch. With a corporation, the business continues with all of the same licenses, bank accounts, etc.

☞ If one partner dies, a partnership may be forced out of business. The surviving heirs can force the sale of their share of the assets of the partnership, even if the remaining partner needs them to continue the business. If he does not have the money to buy-out the heirs, the business may have to be dissolved. With a corporation, the heirs would only inherit stock. With properly drawn documents, the business could continue.

EASE OF
TRANSFERABILITY

A corporation and all of its assets and accounts may be transferred by the simple assignment of a stock certificate. With a sole proprietorship or partnership, each of the individual assets must be transferred and the accounts, licenses, and permits must be individually transferred.

Example:

☞ If a sole proprietorship is sold, the new owner will have to get a new license (if one is required), set up his own bank account, apply for a new federal taxpayer identification number, and new state tax account numbers. The title to any vehicles and real estate will have to be put in his name and all open accounts will have to be changed to his name. He will probably have to submit new credit applications. With a corporation, all of these items remain in the same corporate name. **Note:** In some cases, the new owners will have to submit personal applications for such things as credit or liquor licenses.

OWNERSHIP CAN BE TRANSFERRED WITHOUT CONTROL

By distributing stock, the owner of a business can share the profits of a business without giving up control.

Example:

☞ If an individual wants to give his children some of the profits of his business, he can give them stock and pay dividends to them without giving any management control. This would not be possible with a partnership or sole proprietorship.

EASE OF RAISING CAPITAL

A corporation may raise capital by selling stock or borrowing money. A corporation does not pay taxes on money it raises by the sale of stock.

Example:

☞ If a corporation wants to expand, the owners can sell off ten, twenty-five, or forty-five percent of the stock and still remain in control of the business. Many individuals considering investing may be more willing to invest if they know they will have a piece of the action.

Note: There are strict rules about the sale of stock with criminal penalties and triple damages for violators. (see Chapter 5.)

SEPARATE RECORD KEEPING

A corporation is required to keep its bank accounts and records separate from the accounts of its stockholders, whereas a sole proprietor or partnership may mix business and personal accounts, a practice that often causes confusion in record keeping and is not recommended.

TAX ADVANTAGES

There are several tax advantages that are available only to corporations.

Examples:

☞ Medical insurance for families may be fully deductible.

☞ A tax deferred trust can be set up for a retirement plan.

☞ Losses are fully deductible for a corporation, whereas an individual must prove there was a profit motive before deducting losses.

EASE OF ESTATE PLANNING

Shares of a company can be distributed more easily with a corporation than with a partnership. Heirs can be given different percentages and control can be limited to the appropriate parties.

PRESTIGE

The name of a corporation often sounds more prestigious than the name of a sole proprietor. John Smith d/b/a Acme Builders sounds like a lone man. Acme Builders, Incorporated, sounds as if it might be a large operation. It has been suggested that an individual who is president of a corporation looks more successful than one doing business in their own name. The appearance of a business starts with its name.

SEPARATE CREDIT RATING

A corporation has its own credit rating that may be better or worse than the shareholder's personal credit rating. A corporate business can go bankrupt and the shareholder's personal credit will remain unharmed. Conversely, one shareholder's credit may be bad but the corporation will maintain a good rating For example, if one shareholder gets a judgment against him, this would usually not affect the business of the corporation, whereas it could put an end to a business that was a partnership.

DISADVANTAGES

EXTRA TAX RETURN & ANNUAL REPORT

A corporation is required to file its own tax return. This is a bit longer and more complicated than the form required for a sole proprietorship or partnership. Additional expenses for the services of an accountant may be required. Typically, a corporation must also file a simple annual report with the state (which lists names and addresses of officers and directors) and pay a fee.

SEPARATE RECORDS

The shareholders of a corporation must be careful to keep their personal business separate from the business of the corporation. The corporation must have its own records, keep minutes of meetings, and keep all corporate money separate from personal money.

EXTRA
EXPENSES

There are additional expenses in operating a corporation. People who employ an attorney to form their corporation pay a lot more than people who use this book. Also, in some states a shareholder may have to pay unemployment or worker's compensation insurance covering himself which he wouldn't have to pay as a sole proprietor.

CHECKING
ACCOUNTS

Under federal law, checks made out to a corporation cannot be cashed by a shareholder. They must be deposited into a corporate account. Some banks have higher fees just for businesses that are incorporated.

LEGAL
REPRESENTATION

Unlike a sole proprietor or partners who can represent themselves in court proceedings, a corporation usually must be represented by an attorney. This may not be necessary in small claims court.

CORPORATIONS COMPARED TO LLCs

Limited Liability companies are the newest type of business entity. Like corporations, they offer many benefits over partnerships and sole proprietorships. Whether an LLC or a corporation is better for a small business depends on the type of business.

CORPORATION
ADVANTAGES

The main advantage of an S corporation over an LLC is that with an S corporation, profits taken out other than salary are not subject to social security and medicare taxes (15.3% at the time of publication).

For a large business where the owners take out salaries of $65,000 or more plus profits, there would not be much difference since the social security tax cuts out at about that level. But for a smaller business, where an owner could take out a $30,000 salary and $20,000 profit, the extra taxes on the $20,000 would be over $3,000.

Also, if a corporation plans to go public or sell stock to a large group of people, the corporate stock might be easier to sell than membership interests in the LLC.

LLC
ADVANTAGES

The main advantages of LLCs are found in certain tax situations. For example, an LLC can make special allocations of profits and losses among members, whereas S corporations cannot. S corporations must have one class of ownership in which profits and losses are allocated according to the percentage ownership. In an LLC, money borrowed by the company can increase the tax basis of the owners (and lower the taxes), whereas in an S corporation, it does not. Contributing property to set up an LLC is not taxable, even for minority interest owners, whereas for a corporation regulations only allow it to be tax free for the contributors who have control of the business. (IRC §351.)

The owners of an LLC can be foreign persons, other corporations, or any kind of trust, whereas the owners of S corporations cannot be. An LLC may have an unlimited number of members, while an S corporation is limited to 75.

WHICH TYPE OF CORPORATION IS BEST?

3

DOMESTIC CORPORATION OR FOREIGN CORPORATION

A person wishing to form a corporation must decide whether the corporation will be a *domestic* corporation or a *foreign* corporation. A domestic corporation is one formed in the state in which it is doing business, a foreign corporation is one incorporated in another state or country.

DELAWARE CORPORATIONS — In the past there was some advantage to incorporating in Delaware, since that state had very liberal laws regarding corporations. Many national corporations are incorporated there. However, in recent years, most states have liberalized their corporation laws—so today there is no advantage to incorporating in Delaware for most people.

NEVADA CORPORATIONS — Nevada has liberalized its corporation laws recently to attract businesses. It allows bearer stock and other rules that allow more privacy to corporate participants. It also does not share information with the Internal Revenue Service and does not have a state income tax.

If you form a corporation in a state other than the one in which your business is located, you will be required to have an agent or an office in that state, and you will have to register as a foreign corporation doing business in your state. This is more expensive and more complicated than incorporating in your own state. Also, if you are sued by someone who is not in your state, they can sue you in the state in which you are incorporated, which would probably be more expensive for you than a suit filed in your local court. In some states, your corporation may be required to pay state income tax.

DOUBLE INCORPORATION

One way that a Nevada, Delaware, or other corporation can be useful is if your state has high income taxes. By using two corporations, you could transfer your profits to a state which has no income tax.

For example, suppose you were a painting contractor who owned a building and equipment. You could incorporate in your home state as a painting contractor, but put the building and equipment into a Nevada corporation. The Nevada corporation would then lease these to the local corporation. After paying the workers, buying supplies, paying you a salary, and making lease payments to the Nevada corporation, your local company could break even with no taxable profit. The profit would all be in the Nevada corporation which does not pay taxes in your state.

From a federal tax standpoint there would seldom be an issue because taxes would have to be paid on the profits whichever corporation they were in.

From a state tax standpoint there would be a couple of issues. One is whether the Nevada corporation was "doing business" in your state. If the acts of the Nevada corporation are passive enough, it might not even need to register as doing business in your state. For example, if it just loaned money to your corporation, it would not have to register (especially if you happened to go to Las Vegas to sign the papers). In most states, merely owning rental real estate does not require a corporation to register.

A second issue would be whether your state has any "catch-all" tax laws which would prevent this kind of setup. If you are going to set up two corporations for this purpose, you should meet with a local tax specialist to be sure that it is done correctly under your state requirements.

S-CORPORATION OR C-CORPORATION

A corporation has a choice of how it wants to be taxed. It can make the election at the beginning of its existence or at the beginning of a new tax year. The choices are as follows:

S-CORPORATION   Formerly called a "Subchapter S corporation," an S-corporation pays no income tax and may only be used for small businesses. All of the income or losses of the corporation for the year are passed through to the shareholders who report them on their individual returns. At the end of each year the corporation files an "information return" listing all of its income, expenses, depreciation, etc., and sends each shareholder a notice of his or her share as determined by percentage of stock ownership.

Advantages. Using this method avoids double taxation and allows the pass-through of losses and depreciation. For tax purposes, the business is treated as a partnership. Since many businesses have tax losses during the initial years due to start-up costs, many businesses elect S status and switch over to C-corporation status in later years. Be aware that once a corporation terminates its S status, there is a waiting period before it can switch back. Typically, S-corporations do not have to pay state corporate income tax.

Disadvantages. If stockholders are in high income brackets, their share of the profits will be taxed at those rates. Shareholders who do not "materially participate" in the business cannot deduct losses. Some fringe benefits such as health and life insurance may not be tax deductible.

Requirements. To qualify for S-corporation status, the corporation must:

☞   have no more than seventy-five shareholders, none of whom are non-resident aliens or corporations, all of whom consent to the election, (shares owned by a husband and wife jointly are considered owned by one shareholder),

☞   have only one class of stock,

☞   not be a member of an "affiliated group,"

15

- ☞ generate at least twenty percent of its income in this country and have no more than twenty percent of its income from "passive" sources (interest, rents, dividends, royalties, securities transactions), and

- ☞ file Form 2553 with the IRS before the end of the fifteenth day of the third month of the tax year for which it is to be effective and be approved by the IRS. Approval is usually routine.

C-CORPORATION

A C-corporation pays taxes on its net earnings at corporate rates. Salaries of officers, directors, and employees are taxable to them and deductible to the corporation. However, money paid out in dividends is taxed twice. It is taxed at the corporation's rate as part of its profit, and then at the individual stockholders' rates as income, when distributed by the corporation to them.

Advantages. If taxpayers are in a higher tax bracket than the corporation and the money will be left in the company for expansion, taxes are saved. Fringe benefits such as health, accident, and life insurance are deductible expenses.

Disadvantages. Double taxation of dividends by the federal government can be a big disadvantage. Also, most states have an income tax that only applies to C-corporations and applies to all income over a certain amount. **Note:** Neither of these taxes applies to money taken out as salaries, and many small business owners take all profits out as salaries to avoid double taxation and state income tax. But there are rules requiring that salaries be reasonable. If a stockholder's salary is deemed to be too high relative to his job, the salary may be considered to be partially a dividend and subject to double taxation.

Requirements. None. All corporations are C-corporations unless they specifically elect to become S-corporations.

CLOSELY HELD CORPORATION ELECTION

A closely held corporation election is beneficial for many small businesses. It's purpose is to place restrictions on the transferability of stock. Often it obligates a shareholder to offer to the corporation or the shareholders the opportunity to purchase the stock before offering it to any outside purchaser. If the corporation and shareholders reject the offer, they typically must still consent to who the transferee (buyer) of the shares will be.

To elect to have these restrictions, they should be included in the bylaws, printed on the certificates, and in many states they must be included in the articles of incorporation.

INC. OR P.A./ P.C.

Under the laws of most states, certain types of services can only be rendered by a corporation if it is a *professional association* ("P.A."), or *professional service corporation* ("P.C."). These include such professionals as attorneys, physicians, certified public accountants, veterinarians, architects, life insurance agents, and chiropractors. For simplicity, these will be referred to as *professional service corporations*. A professional service corporation typically has specific rules under the state incorporation statutes.

PURPOSE   A professional service corporation must usually have one specific purpose spelled out in the articles of incorporation and that purpose must be to practice a specific profession. It may not engage in any other business, but it may invest its funds in real estate, stocks, bonds, mortgages, or other types of investments. A professional service corporation may change its purpose to another legal purpose, but it will then no longer be a professional service corporation.

NAME   In most states, the name of a professional service corporation must contain the word "chartered," "professional association," or "professional corporation," or the abbreviation "P.A." or "P.C." Typically, it may not use the words "company," "corporation" or "incorporated" or any abbreviation of these. (see Appendix A.)

SHAREHOLDERS   According to the law in most states, only persons licensed to practice a profession may be shareholders of a professional service corporation engaged in that practice. A shareholder who loses the right to practice must immediately sever all employment with, and financial interests in, such a corporation. If such a shareholder does not, the corporation may be dissolved by the state. No shareholder may enter into a voting trust or other similar arrangement with anyone.

MERGER A professional service corporation may not merge with any other corporation except a professional service corporation which is licensed to perform the same type of service.

REQUIREMENTS Most states have very specific requirements for the formation of professional service corporations. They often require specific language in the articles, charter, or bylaws. For this type of corporation you should consult an attorney or obtain a copy of your state statute on professional corporations.

NOT-FOR-PROFIT CORPORATIONS

Not-for-profit corporations are usually used for social clubs, churches, and charities, and are beyond the scope of this book. While they are similar to for-profit corporations in many aspects, such as limited liability and the required formalities, there are additional state and federal requirements which must be met.

In some cases, a business can be formed as a not-for-profit corporation. It would not be allowed to distribute profits to its founders but it could pay substantial salaries and enjoy numerous tax advantages. For information on books dealing with not-for-profit corporations, check your local bookstore or library.

START-UP PROCEDURES 4

NAME SEARCH

The first thing to do before starting a corporation is to thoroughly check out the name you wish to use to be sure it is not already being used by someone else. Many businesses have been forced to stop using their name after spending thousands of dollars promoting it.

CORPORATE RECORDS

The first place to check is your Secretary of State's office to see if the name has already been used by another corporation in your state. To do this you can write or call their office. See Appendix A for phone numbers and addresses. In some states you can access your state's corporate records through the internet and conduct your own search of all current and dissolved corporations. Some of the web sites are included in Appendix A. If your state's records are not listed or have changed, you may be able to access it through the following site which has listings for all states:

http://www.findlaw.com/11stategov/index.html

FICTITIOUS NAMES

Besides checking corporate names, you should check if another business is using the name you want as a fictitious name. In some states these are registered with each county and in others they are registered with the

Secretary of State. Some states that register the names with the Secretary of State can be searched over the internet as described above.

BUSINESS
LISTINGS

Since some businesses neglect to properly register their name (yet still may have superior rights to the name) you should also check phone books and business directories. Many libraries have phone books from around the country as well as directories of trade names.

YELLOW PAGE
LISTINGS

If you have a computer with Internet access you can search every yellow pages listing for free. Just search for "yellow pages" with any web search engine (i.e., Yahoo, WebCrawler, Lycos, etc.) You can select a state, enter your business name, and it will tell you if any other companies are listed with that name. One site that allows you to search all states at once is:

http://www.switchboard.com

If you do not have access to a computer, you may be able to use one at your public library or have the search done at your library for a small fee.

TRADEMARK
SEARCH

To be sure that you are not violating a registered trademark, you should have a search done of the records of the United States Patent and Trademark Office. In the past, this required a visit to their offices or the hiring of a search firm for over a hundred dollars. But in 1999, the USPTO put its trademark records online and you can now search them at: http://www.uspto.gov/tmdb/index.html.

If you do not have access to the Internet, you might be able to do it at a public library or, for a small fee, have one of their employees order an online search for you. You can have the search done through a firm if this is not available to you. Some firms that do searches are:

Government Liaison Services, Inc.
3030 Clarendon Blvd., Suite 209
P. O. Box 10648
Arlington, VA 22210
(800) 642-6564; (703) 524-8200

Thomson & Thomson
500 Victory Road
North Quincy, MA 02171-1545
(800) 692-8833

XL Corporate Service
62 White Street
New York, NY 10013
(800) 221-2972

NAME
RESERVATION

It is possible to reserve a name for a corporation for a certain period of time by filing a reservation form and paying the appropriate fee (see Appendix A for your state's information). However, this is usually pointless because it is just as easy to file the articles, as it is to reserve the name. One possible reason for reserving a name would be to hold it while waiting for a trademark name search to arrive.

SIMILAR NAMES

Sometimes it seems as if every good name is taken. But a name can often be modified slightly or used on a different type of product or service. Try different variations if your favorite is taken. Another possibility is to give the corporation one name and then do business under a fictitious name. (see FICTITIOUS NAMES on page 19.)

Example:

☞ If you want to use the name "Flowers by Freida" in Pensacola and there is already a "Flowers by Freida, Inc." in Miami, you might incorporate under the name "Freida Jones, Inc." and then register the corporation as doing business under the fictitious name "Flowers by Freida." Unless "Flowers by Freida, Inc." has registered a trademark for the name either in Florida or nationally, you will probably be able to use the name. **Note:** You should realize that you might run into complications later, especially if you decide to expand into other areas of the state or other states. One protection available would be to register the name as a trademark. This would give you exclusive use of the name anywhere that it was not already being used.

FORBIDDEN
NAMES

A corporation may not use certain words in its name if there would be a likelihood of confusion. There are state and federal laws that control the use of these words. In most cases your application will be rejected if you use a forbidden word. Some of the words which may not be used in some states without special licenses or registration are:

Assurance	Disney
Bank	Insurance
Banker	Olympic
Banking	Trust
Credit Union	

If you use a word that is forbidden, then your papers will most likely be returned. You may wish to call the corporate registrar to ask if the name you plan to use is allowed.

TRADEMARKS

The name of a business may not be registered as a trademark, but a name used on goods or to sell services may be registered, and such registration will grant the holder exclusive rights to use that name except in areas where someone else has used the name. A trademark may be registered both in your state and in the United States Patent and Trademark Office.

Each trademark is registered for a certain "class" of goods. Thus you may usually register the name "Zapata" chewing gum even if someone has registered the name "Zapata" for use on shoes. One exception to this rule is if the name is so well known that your use would cause confusion. For example, you could not use "Coca-Cola" as a brand of shoes because people are so familiar with the Coca-Cola company that they might think the company started a line of shoes. If you want to register the mark for several types of goods or services, you must register it for each different class into which the goods or services fall, and pay a separate fee for each category.

For protection within each state, the mark may be registered with the Department of State. The cost varies from state to state. Application forms and instructions can be obtained through the same department.

For protection across the entire United States, the mark can be registered with the United States Patent and Trademark Office and the fee is $325 at the time of publication of this book. The procedure for federal registration is more complicated than state registration and is explained in the book *How to Register Your Own Trademark* available from the publisher of this book, or at your local bookstore.

FICTITIOUS NAMES
A corporation may operate under a fictitious or assumed name just as an individual can. This is done when a corporation wants to operate several businesses under different names or if the business name is not available as a corporate name. Fictitious names are either registered in each county or are registered statewide with the Secretary of State. However, registering a fictitious name does not give the registrant any rights to the name. While corporate names are carefully checked by the Secretary of State and disallowed if they are similar to others, in many states fictitious names are filed without checking and any number of people may register the same name. The cost of registering a fictitious name varies. Application forms and instructions can be obtained from your local courthouse or Secretary of State's office.

Note: When a fictitious name is used by a corporation, the corporate name should also be used. This is because if the public does not see that they are dealing with a corporation, they may be able to "pierce the corporate veil" and sue the stockholders individually. Thus all signs, business cards, etc., should list the names in one of the following ways:

Smith Enterprises, Inc. d/b/a Internet Resources

or

Internet Resources, a division of Smith Enterprises, Inc.

ARTICLES OF INCORPORATION

To create a corporation, a document must be filed with the state agency that keeps corporate records, which in most states is the Secretary of State. In most states, this document is called the Articles of Incorporation; however, in some states, it may be called the "Certificate of Incorporation," "Articles of Association," or the "Charter." This document is referred to as the *Articles of Incorporation* throughout this book. Some corporations have long, elaborate articles that describe numerous powers and functions, but most of this is unnecessary. The powers of corporations are explained in state law and do not have to be repeated. Some attorneys prepare long articles of incorporation, however, short articles are just as legal and allow more flexibility.

Typically, state law requires only a minimum amount of detail be included in the Articles of Incorporation. Some things, such as the purpose of the corporation, regulations for the operation of the corporation, and a par value of the stock may be explained in the articles of incorporation. This is not advisable unless required, since any changes would necessitate the complicated process of amending the articles. It is better to explain these terms in the bylaws. The matters typically required to be contained in the articles and a few of the optional provisions are:

Name of the corporation. Most states require that the corporation name contain one of the following six words:

- Incorporated
- Inc.
- Corporation
- Corp.
- Company
- Co.

(The specific name requirements for your state are listed in Appendix A.)

The reason for the requirement is so that persons dealing with the business will be on notice that it is a corporation. This is important in protecting the shareholders from liability.

Address of the corporation. The street address of the principal office and the mailing address of the corporation must be provided.

The number of shares of stock the corporation is authorized to issue. This is usually an even number such as 100, 1000 or 1,000,000.

In some cases it may be advantageous to issue different classes of stock, such as common and preferred, or voting and non-voting, but such matters should be discussed with an attorney or accountant.

If there are different classes of stock, then the articles of incorporation must contain a designation of the classes and a statement of the preferences, limitations, and relative rights of each class. In addition, if there are to be any preferred or special shares issued in series, then the articles must explain the relative rights and preferences and any authority of the board of directors to establish preferences. Any preemptive rights must also be explained.

This book will explain how to form a corporation with one class of stock. It is usually advisable to authorize double or quadruple the amount of stock which will be initially issued. The unissued stock can be issued later if more capital is contributed by a shareholder or by a new member of the business.

One important point to keep in mind when issuing stock relates to par value. Par value is the total number of shares that a corporation may issue under its Articles divided by the total initial investment in the corporation. Par value is not always the actual value of the stock because a corporation's net worth may play a role. When issuing stock, the full par value must be paid for in shares. If this is not done, then the shareholder can later be held liable for the full par value. For more important information about issuing stock see Chapter 5.

The name of the registered agent and the address of the registered office along with the agent's acceptance. Each corporation must have a registered agent and a registered office. The registered office can be the business office of the corporation if the registered agent works out of that office, it can be the office of another individual who is the registered agent (such as an attorney), or it may be a corporate registered agent's office. Technically it may not be a residence unless that address is also a business office of the corporation. Penalty for failure to comply can be the inability to maintain a lawsuit and a possible fine.

The name and address of the incorporator of the corporation. This may be any person, even if that person has no future interest in the corporation. There are companies in state capitols that will, on a moment's notice, have someone run over to the Secretary of State to file corporate articles that are later assigned to the real parties in interest. However, in some states, those who maintain deposits of funds with the Secretary of State are allowed to file articles by facsimile, so there is less need to run these days.

Duration. In most states, the duration of the corporation need not be mentioned if it is to be perpetual. If not, the duration must be specified in the articles.

Effective date. A specific effective date may be in the articles but is not required. Articles are effective upon filing. If an effective date is specified, state law varies as to the time before or after the filing in which the Articles of Incorporation are effective.

EXECUTION   The Articles of Incorporation must be signed by the incorporator and dated. Typically, the registered agent must sign a statement accepting his duties as such. This is sometimes done as a separate form or sometimes on the same form as the articles.

FORMS   Articles of Incorporation need not be on any certain form. They can be typed on blank paper or can be on a fill-in-the-blank form. In Appendix B of this book are forms of Articles of Incorporation for each state. Some states have their own incorporation forms which you can get by mail or over the Internet. The addresses, phone numbers and Internet addresses are in Appendix A.

FILING   The Articles of Incorporation must be filed with the Secretary of State by sending them to the address listed in Appendix A along with the filing fees. The fees (as available at time of publication) are listed in Appendix A as well. If you wish to receive a certified copy of the articles, the cost is additional. In many states this is an unnecessary expense since a certified copy is rarely, if ever, needed. Ask your bank if a certified copy will be required by it. Usually the better alternative is to enclose a photocopy along with the articles and ask that it be "stamped with the filing date" and returned. See Appendix C for a letter to the Secretary of State.

In most states the return time for the articles is usually a week or two. If there is a need to have them back quickly, you might be able to send them and have them returned by a courier such as Federal Express, Airborne Express, or UPS with prepaid return. Call your Secretary of State for details.

SHAREHOLDER AGREEMENT

When there are two or more shareholders in a corporation, they should consider drawing up a shareholder agreement. This document explains what is to happen in the event of a disagreement between the parties. In closely held corporations the minority shareholders have a risk of being locked into a long term enterprise with little or no way to withdraw their capital. A shareholder agreement is a fairly complicated document and should be drawn up by an attorney. This may be costly but the expense should be weighed against the costs of lengthy litigation should the parties break up. Some of the things which may be addressed in such an agreement are as follows:

- Veto by minority shareholder
- Greater than majority voting requirement
- Cumulative voting

- Deadlocks
- Arbitration
- Dissolution
- Compulsory buy-out
- Preemptive rights
- Restrictions on transfers of shares
- Refusal of a party to participate

ORGANIZATIONAL PAPERWORK

Every corporation must have bylaws and must maintain a set of minutes of its meetings. The bylaws must be adopted at the first meeting and the first minutes of the corporation will record the proceedings of the organizational meeting.

WAIVER OF
NOTICE

Before any meeting of the incorporators, board of directors, or shareholders can be held, formal notice must be given to the parties of the meeting. Since small corporations often need to have meetings on short notice and do not want to be bothered with formal notices, it is customary to have all parties sign written waivers of notice. Waivers of notice are included in the book for the organizational meeting and for the annual and special meetings (see Appendix C).

BYLAWS

The bylaws are the rules for organization and operation of the corporation. They are required by state law. Appendix C contains one form of bylaws for a simple corporation. To complete it, fill in the name and state of the corporation, the city of the main office of the corporation, the proposed date of the annual meeting (this can be varied each year as needed), and the number of directors to be on the board.

MINUTES

As part of the formal requirements of operating a corporation, minutes must be kept of the meetings of shareholders and the board of directors. Usually only one meeting of each is required each year unless there is some special need for a meeting in the interim (such as the resignation of an officer). The first minutes will be the minutes of the organizational meeting of the corporation. At this meeting the officers and directors are elected, the bylaws, corporate seal, and stock certificates are adopted and other organizational decisions made. Most of the forms are self-explanatory. (see Appendix C.)

RESOLUTIONS

When the board of directors or shareholders make major decisions it is usually done in the form of a resolution. At the organizational meeting some important resolutions which may be passed are choosing a bank and adopting S-corporation status (see Appendix C).

TAX FORMS

FORM SS-4
(EMPLOYER
IDENTIFICATION
NUMBER)

Prior to opening a bank account, the corporation must obtain an *Employer Identification Number* that is the corporate equivalent of a social security number. This is done by filing Form SS-4 which is included in this book in Appendix C. This usually takes two or three weeks, so it should be filed early. Send the form to your local Internal Revenue Service Center.

If you need the identification number quickly, you may be able to obtain it by calling the IRS. The number for the local office which handles these is in the instructions. Be sure to have your SS-4 form complete before calling and have it in front of you.

When you apply for this number you will probably be put on the mailing list for other corporate tax forms. If you do not receive these, you should call your local IRS office and request the forms for new businesses. These include *Circular E* explaining the taxes due, W-4 forms for each employee, tax deposit coupons, and Form 941 quarterly return for withholding.

FORM 2553
(S-CORPORATION)

If your corporation is to be taxed as an S-corporation, you must file Form 2553 with the IRS within seventy-five days of incorporation. As a practical matter you should sign and file this at your incorporation meeting, otherwise you may forget. This form is included in this book in Appendix C.

STATE TAX
FORMS

In most states there is a state corporate income tax. In some states you will be exempt from corporate income tax if you are an S-corporation, but you will need to file a form to let them know that you are exempt.

If you will be selling or renting goods or services at retail, you may be required to collect state sales and use taxes. To do this you will need to register and in most cases pay a registration fee. In some states and in some businesses you will be required to post a bond covering the taxes you will be collecting. There may be other taxes that your state requires. Contact your state taxing authority and ask for the forms available for new corporations.

CORPORATE SUPPLIES

CORPORATE
KITS

A corporation needs to keep a permanent record of its legal affairs. This includes: the original articles of incorporation; minutes of all meetings; records of the stock issued, transferred and cancelled; fictitious names registered; and any other legal matters. The records are usually kept in a ring binder. Any ring binder will do, but it is possible to purchase a specially prepared "corporate kit" which has the name of the corporation printed on it and usually contains forms such as minutes and stock certificates. Most of these items are included with this book, so purchasing such a kit is unnecessary unless you want to have a fancy leather binder or specially printed stock certificates.

Some sources for corporate kits are:

Ace Industries, Inc.
54 NW 11th St.
Miami, FL 33136-9978
(305) 358-2571
(800) 433-2571

Midstate Legal Supply Co., Inc.
P. O. Box 2122
Orlando, FL 32802
(407) 299-8220
(800) 327-9220

Corpex
1440 5th Ave.
Bayshore, NY 11106
(800) 221-8181

CORPORATE
SEAL

One thing that is not included with this book is a corporate seal. This must be specially made for each corporation. Most corporations use a metal seal like a notary's seal to emboss the paper. This can be ordered from an office supply company. Some states now allow rubber stamps for corporate seals. These are cheaper, lighter and easier to read. Rubber stamp seals can also be ordered from office supply stores, printers and specialized rubber stamp companies. The corporate seal should contain the full, exact name of the corporation, the word "SEAL" and the year of incorporation. It may be round or rectangular.

STOCK
CERTIFICATES &
OFFERS TO
PURCHASE STOCK

In some states, corporations are no longer required to issue stock certificates to represent shares of ownership. However, as a practical matter it is a good idea to do so. This shows some formality and gives each person tangible evidence of ownership. If you do issue shares, the face of each certificate must show the corporate name, the state law under which the corporation was organized, the name of the shareholder(s), and the number, class and series of the stock. The certificate must be signed by one or more officers designated by the bylaws or the board of directors.

If there are two or more classes or series of stock, the front or back of the certificate must disclose that, upon request and without charge, the corporation will provide to the shareholder the preferences, limitations and relative rights of each class or series, the preferences of any preferred stock, and the board of directors' authority to determine rights for any subsequent classes or series. If there are any restrictions, they must be stated on the certificate or a statement must be included that a copy of the restrictions is available without charge.

The stock certificates can be fancy and intricately engraved with eagles and scrolls, or they can be typed or even handwritten. If you purchase a "corporate kit" then you will receive certificates printed with your company's name on them. Ready-to-use stock certificates are included in this book.

Before any stock is issued, the purchaser should submit an "Offer to Purchase Stock" (see Form G in Appendix C.) The Offer states that it is made pursuant to IRS Code §1244. (Internal Revenue Code, section 1244.) The advantage of this section is that in the event the business fails or the value of the stock drops, the shareholder can write off up to $50,000 ($100,000 for married couples) as ordinary income, rather than as a long term capital loss which would be limited to $3,000 a year.

Some thought should be given to the way in which the ownership of the stock will be held. Stock owned in one person's name alone is subject to probate upon death. Making two persons joint owners of the stock (joint tenants with full rights of survivorship) would avoid probate upon the death of one of them. However, taking a joint owner's name off in the event of a disagreement (such as divorce) could be troublesome. Where a couple jointly operates a business, joint ownership would be best. But where one person is the sole party involved in the business, the desire to avoid probate should be weighed against the risk of losing half the business in a divorce.

A new law has been drafted recently which allows securities to be registered in "pay on death" or "transfer on death" form, similar to bank accounts. This means the stock can be owned by one person, but designated to pass to another person at death without that person getting any current rights in the stock. At the time of publication of this book the law has been passed by twenty-seven states, but others may pass it in the future. Check with your stock broker, attorney, or in your state statutes. The law is called the Uniform TOD Securities Registration Act. The following states have passed it at the time of completion of this manuscript:

Alaska	Illinois	New Jersey	Utah
Arizona	Kansas	New Mexico	Virginia
Arkansas	Maryland	North Dakota	Washington
Colorado	Michigan	Ohio	West Virginia
Delaware	Minnesota	Oklahoma	Wisconsin
Florida	Montana	Oregon	Wyoming
Idaho	Nebraska	South Dakota	

TAXES   Some states levy a tax on the issue or transfer of stock. The amount and means of calculating the tax vary from state to state. Check with the Secretary of State or your county government tax office to find out if any such tax is charged, how to calculate the amount of tax, and how to go about paying it.

This is a tax you can easily lower, but do not avoid paying it. If you do, someone may use this to pierce the corporate veil and hold you liable for debts of the corporation.

You can keep the tax low by structuring your corporate stock to the minimum tax. In some states this means fewer shares, in other states it means lower par value.

To compare two states, in Ohio the tax is on the number of shares. To keep the tax low you would issue a small number of shares and pay a higher amount for each share. In Florida, the tax is based on the payment for the shares, so you could issue a large number of shares with a low par value. If you wanted to contribute more capital to the corporation, you should designate it as "paid-in surplus" rather than as payment for more shares.

The Ohio tax is ten cents per share for the first 1,000 shares with a minimum tax of eight-five dollars. This means you can have 850 shares without paying extra tax. A person forming an Ohio corporation with $5,000 in capital could authorize 850 shares at two dollars par value, issue 500 and pay ten dollars per share.

Florida does not have a tax on authorized shares but has a documentary stamp tax on issued shares. Thus you could authorize 1,000,000 shares at $0.001 par value and pay $1000 for all 1,000,000 shares. Additional capital could be contributed as paid-in surplus or as a loan to the corporation.

ORGANIZATIONAL MEETING

The real birth of the corporation takes place at the initial meeting of the incorporators and the initial board of directors. At this meeting the stock is issued and the officers and board of directors are elected. Other business may also take place, such as opting for S-corporation status or adopting employee benefit plans.

Usually, minutes, stock certificates, tax and other forms are prepared before the organizational meeting and used as a script for the meeting. They are then signed at the end of the meeting.

Those items in the following agenda designated with an asterisk (*) are forms found in Appendix C of this book. These forms may be cut out of the book, photocopied, or rewritten as necessary to fit your situation.

The agenda for the initial meeting is usually as follows:

1. Signing the Waiver of Notice of the Meeting*

2. Noting Persons Present

3. Presentation and Acceptance of Articles of Incorporation (the copy returned by the Secretary of State)*

4. Election of Directors

5. Adoption of Bylaws*

6. Election of Officers

7. Presentation and Acceptance of Corporate Seal

8. Presentation and Acceptance of Stock Certificates*

9. Adoption of Banking Resolution*

10. Adoption of Resolution Accepting Stock Offers* (Use Form H, Bill of Sale, if property is traded for stock.)

11. Adoption of Resolution to Pay Expenses*

12. Adoption of Special Resolutions such as S-Corp. Status*

13. Adjournment

The stock certificates are usually issued at the end of the meeting, but in some cases, such as when a prospective shareholder does not yet have money to pay for them, they are issued when paid for.

To issue the stock, the certificates at the end of this book should be completed by adding the name of the corporation, the state of incorporation, the number of shares the certificate represents and the person to whom the certificate is issued. Each certificate should be numbered in order to keep track of it. A record of the stock issuance should be made on the stock transfer ledger and on the "stubs." (see Appendix C.) The stubs should be cut apart on the dotted lines, punched, and inserted in the ring binder. Some states may charge taxes or fees upon the issuance of stock. You should check with your Secretary of State's office to determine all necessary taxes or fees. (see Appendix A.)

MINUTE BOOK

After the organizational meeting you should set up your minute book. As noted previously, this can be a fancy leather book or a simple ring binder. The minute book usually contains the following:

1. Title page ("Corporate Records of _____")
2. Table of contents
3. The letter from the Secretary of State acknowledging receipt and filing of the Articles of Incorporation
4. Copy of the Articles of Incorporation
5. Copy of any fictitious name registration
6. Copy of any trademark registration
7. Waiver of Notice of Organizational Meeting
8. Minutes of Organizational Meeting
9. Bylaws
10. Sample stock certificate
11. Offer to purchase stock

12. Tax forms:

   a. Form SS-4 and Employer Identification Number

   b. Form 2553 and acceptance

   c. Any State form necessary along with State tax number

13. Stock ledger

14. Stock stubs

BANK ACCOUNT

A corporation will need a bank account. Typically, checks payable to a corporation cannot be cashed by a shareholder; they must be deposited into an account.

BANK
FEES

Unfortunately many banks charge ridiculous rates to corporations for the right to put their money in the bank. You can tell how much extra a corporation is being charged when you compare a corporate account with a personal account with similar activity.

Usually there is a complicated scheme of fees with charges for each transaction. Some banks are even bold enough to charge companies for making a deposit! (Twenty-five cents for the deposit plus ten cents for each check that is deposited. Deposit thirty checks and this will cost you $3.25!) Often the customer is granted an interest credit on the balance in the account, but this is usually small and if the credit is larger than the charges, you lose the excess.

Fortunately, some banks have set up reasonable fees for small corporations. Some charge no fees if a balance of $1,000 or $2,500 is maintained. Because the fees can easily amount to hundreds of dollars a year, it pays to shop around. Even if the bank is relatively far from the business, using bank-by-mail can make the distance meaningless. But don't be surprised if a bank with low fees raises them. The author knows of one company that had to change banks four times in one year as each one raised its fees or was bought out by a bank with higher fees.

Although the banking industry has emerged from the problems of the last decade and are making record profits, fewer banks are offering reasonable fees for corporate checking accounts. But you can usually find loopholes if you use your imagination. One trick is to open a checking account and a money market account. (Money market accounts typically pay higher interest and do not charge for making deposits. You can only write about three checks a month but you can usually make unlimited deposits.) Then make all of your deposits into the money market account and just pay bills out of the checking account, transferring funds as needed. Some banks have figured this out and have begun to charge for deposits to money market accounts. However, most stock brokers and mutual funds offer money market accounts with no charge for deposits.

Another way to save money in bank charges is to order checks from a private source rather than through the bank. These are usually much cheaper than the checks the bank offers, because most banks get a commission on check orders. If the bank officer doesn't like the idea when you are opening the account, just wait until your first batch of bank checks runs out and switch over at that time.

PAPERWORK   All you should need to open a corporate bank account is a copy of your Articles of Incorporation and your federal tax identification number and perhaps a business license. Some banks, however, want more and they sometimes don't even know what they want. After opening numerous corporate accounts with only those items, one individual recently encountered a bank employee who wanted "something certified so we know who your officers are. Your attorney will know what to draw up." He explained that he was an attorney and was the president, secretary and treasurer of the corporation and would write out and sign and seal whatever they wanted. The bank employee insisted that it had to be a nice certificate signed by the secretary of the corporation and sealed. So a statement was typed out in legalese, a gold foil seal was put on it and the bank opened the account. If you have trouble opening the account you can use the "Banking Resolution" included with this book in Appendix C or you can make up a similar form.

LICENSES

In some states, counties and municipalities are authorized to levy a license fee or tax on the "privilege" of doing business. Before opening your business you need to find out if any such license is required. Businesses that perform work in several cities, such as builders, may need to obtain a license from each city or county in which they perform work or have an office.

Every state also has laws requiring the licensing of certain types of businesses or professions. Some states regulate more types than others. Just because you didn't need a license in one state is no guarantee that you won't need one if you move to a new state.

Be sure to find out if zoning allows your type of business before buying or leasing property. Usually the licensing departments will check the zoning before issuing your license.

SELLING CORPORATE STOCK 5

SECURITIES LAWS

The issuance of securities is subject to both federal and state securities laws. A *security* is stock in the company (common and preferred) and debt (notes, bonds, etc.). The laws covering securities are so broad that any instrument that represents an investment in an enterprise, where the investor is relying on the efforts of others for profit, is considered a security.Even a promissory note has been held to be a security. Once an investment is determined to involve a security, strict rules apply. There can be criminal penalties and civil damages can also be awarded to purchasers, if the rules are not followed.

The rules are designed to protect people who put up money as an investment in a business. In the stock market crash in the 1930s, many people lost their life savings in swindles, and the government wants to be sure that it won't happen again. Unfortunately, the laws can also make it difficult to raise capital for many honest businesses.

The goal of the laws covering sales of securities is that investors be given full disclosure of the risks involved in an investment. To accomplish this, the law usually requires that the securities must either be registered with the federal Securities and Exchange Commission (SEC) or a similar state regulatory body, and that lengthy disclosure statements be compiled and distributed.

The law is complicated and strict compliance is required. The penalties are so harsh that most lawyers won't handle securities matters. You most likely would not be able to get through the registration process on your own. But, like your decision to incorporate without a lawyer, you may wish to consider some alternatives when attempting to raise capital without a lawyer:

☞ Borrow the money as a personal loan from the friends or relatives. The disadvantage is that you will have to pay them back personally if the business fails. However, you may have to do that anyway if they are close relatives or if you don't follow the securities laws.

☞ Tailor your stock issuance to fall within the exemptions in the securities laws. There are some exemptions in the securities laws for small businesses that may apply to your transaction. (The anti-fraud provisions always apply, even if the transaction is exempt from registration.) Some exemptions are explained below, but you should make at least one appointment with a securities lawyer to be sure you have covered everything and that there have not been any changes in the law. Often you can pay for an hour or so of a securities lawyer's time for $100 or $200 and just ask questions about your plans. He or she can tell you what not to do and what your options are. Then you can make an informed decision.

FEDERAL EXEMPTIONS FROM SECURITIES LAWS

In most situations where one person, a husband and wife, or a few partners run a business, and all parties are active in the enterprise, securities laws do not apply to their issuance of stock to themselves. These are the simple corporations that are the subject of this book. As a practical matter, if your father or aunt wants to put up some money for some stock in your business—you probably won't get in trouble. They probably won't seek triple damages and criminal penalties if your business fails.

However, you may wish to obtain money from additional investors to enable your business to grow. This can be done in many circumstances as long as you follow the rules carefully. In some cases you do not have to file anything with the SEC, but in others you must file a notice.

FEDERAL PRIVATE OFFERING EXEMPTION

If you sell your stock to a small group of people without any advertising you can fall into the private offering exemption.

- All persons to whom offers are made are financially astute, are participants in the business, or have a substantial net worth,

- No advertising or general solicitation is used to promote the stock,

- The number of persons to whom the offers are made is limited,

- The shares are purchased for investment and not for immediate resale,

- The persons to whom the stock is offered are given all relevant information (including financial information) regarding the issuance and the corporation. Again, there are numerous court cases explaining each aspect of these rules, including such questions as what is a "financially astute" person, and

- A filing claiming the exemption is made upon the United States Securities and Exchange Commission.

FEDERAL INTRASTATE OFFERING EXEMPTION

If you only offer your securities to residents of one state, you may be exempt from federal securities laws. This is because federal laws usually only apply to interstate commerce. Intrastate Offering are covered by SEC Rule 147 and if it is followed carefully your sale will be exempt from federal registration.

FEDERAL SMALL
OFFERINGS
EXEMPTIONS

In recent years, the Securities and Exchange Commission (SEC) has liberalized the rules in order to make it easier for business to grow. The SEC has adopted Regulation D, which states that there are three types of exemptions under SEC Rules 504, 505 and 506.

Offering of securities of up to $1,000,000 in a twelve-month period can be exempt under SEC Rule 504. Offers can be made to any number of persons, no specific information must be provided and investors do not have to be sophisticated.

Under SEC Rule 505, offering of up to $5,000,000 can be made in a twelve-month period but no public advertising may be used and only thirty-five non-accredited investors may purchase stock. Any number of accredited investors may purchase stock.

Accredited investors are sophisticated individuals with high net worth or high income, large trusts or investment companies or persons involved in the business.

SEC Rule 506 has no limit on the amount of money that may be raised but, like Rule 505, does not allow advertising and limits non-accredited investors to thirty-five.

STATE SECURITIES LAWS

One reason there are exemptions from federal securities laws is that there are so many state laws covering securities that additional registration is not needed. Every state has securities laws, which are called *blue sky laws*. If you wish to offer your stock in all fifty states you must be registered in all fifty states unless you can fit into one of the exemptions. However, exemptions are very limited.

PRIVATE
PLACEMENT
EXEMPTION

The most common is the private placement exemption. This can apply if all of the following are true:

- There are thirty-five or fewer purchasers of shares.

- No commissions are paid to anyone to promote the stock.

- No advertising or general solicitation is used to promote the stock.

- All material information (including financial information) regarding the stock issuance and the company is given to or accessible to all shareholders.

- A three day right of recision is given.

These rules may sound simple on the surface but there are many more rules, regulations and court cases explaining each one in more detail. For example, what does "thirty-five persons" mean? Sounds simple, but it can mean more than thirty-five persons. Spouses, persons whose net worth exceeds a million dollars, and founders of the corporation may not be counted in some circumstances. Each state has its own *blue sky* requirements and exemptions. If you are going to raise money from investors, check with a qualified securities lawyer.

As you can see, the exemption doesn't give you much latitude in raising money. Therefore you will have to register. To find out more about the registration process in each state you should contact the office in each state in which you intend to sell stock. The addresses are at the end of this chapter.

INTERNET STOCK SALES

With the advent of the Internet, promoters of stock have a new way of reaching large numbers of people financially able to afford investments in securities. However, all securities laws apply to the Internet and they are being enforced. Recently state attorneys general have issued cease and desist orders to promoters not registered in their states.

Under current law you must be registered in a state in order to sell stock to its residents. If you are not registered in a state you must turn down any residents from that state that want to buy your stock.

You may wonder how the famous Spring Street Brewing raised $1.6 million for its Wit Beer on the Internet. The main reason they were successful was perhaps because their president is a lawyer and could prepare his own prospectus to file with the SEC and all fifty states.

PAYMENT FOR SHARES

When issuing stock it is important that full payment be made by the purchasers. If the shares have a par value and the payment is in cash, then the cash must not be less than the par value. In most states promissory notes cannot be used in payment for shares. The shares must not be issued until the payment has been received by the corporation.

TRADING PROPERTY FOR SHARES

In many cases organizers of a corporation have property they want to contribute for use in starting up the business. This is often the case where an on-going business is incorporated. To avoid future problems, the property should be traded at a fair value for the shares. The directors should pass a resolution stating that they agree with the value of the property. When the stock certificate is issued in exchange for the property, a bill of sale should be executed by the owner of the property detailing everything that is being exchanged for the stock.

TAXABLE TRANSACTIONS

In cases where property is exchanged for something of value, such as stock, there is often income tax due as if there had been a sale of the property. Fortunately the Federal Tax Code allows tax-free exchange of property for stock if the persons receiving the stock for the property or for cash *end up owning* at least eighty percent of the voting and other stock in the corporation. (Internal Revenue Service Code, section 351.) If more than twenty percent of the stock is issued in exchange for services instead of property and cash, then the transfers of property will be taxable and treated as a sale for cash.

TRADING
SERVICES FOR
SHARES

In some cases the founders of a corporation wish to issue stock to one or more persons in exchange for their services to the corporation. It has always been possible to issue shares for services that have previously been performed. Some states make it unlawful to issue shares for promises to perform services in the future. Check your corporation's statutes regarding this.

STATE SECURITIES REGISTRATION OFFICES

The following are the addresses of the state offices that handle registration of securities. You can contact them for information on their requirements.

Alabama Securities Commission
770 Washington Avenue, Suite 570
Montgomery, Alabama 36130-4700
Phone: (334) 242-2984
Fax: (334) 242-0240
e-mail: alseccom@dsmd.dsmd.state.al.us

Division of Banking, Securities,
& Corporations
Department of Community and Economic
Development
P.O. Box 110807
150 Third Street, Suite 217
Juneau, AK 99801-0807
Phone: (907) 465-2521
Fax: (907) 465-2549
e-mail: dbsc@dced.state.ak.us
Internet:
http://www.dced.state.ak.us/bsc/secur.htm

Arizona Corporation Commission
1300 West Washington, Third Floor
Phoenix, Arizona 85007
Phone: (602) 542-4242
Fax: (602) 594-7470
e-mail: accsec@ccsd.cc.state.az.us
Internet: http://www.ccsd.cc.state.az.us/

Arkansas Securities Department
Heritage West Building - Room 300
201 East Markham
Little Rock, Arkansas 72201
Phone: (501) 324-9260
Fax: (501) 324-9268
e-mail: securities@mail.state.ar.us
Internet: http://www.state.ar.us/arsec

California Department of Corporations
3700 Wilshire Boulevard
Los Angeles, CA 90010
Phone: (213) 736-3481
Fax: (213) 736-3588
Internet: http://www.corp.ca.gov/srd/
security.htm

Colorado Division of Securities
1580 Lincoln, Suite 420
Denver, Colorado 80203
Phone: (303) 894-2320
Fax: (303) 861-2126 (fax)

e-mail: Securities@DORA.state.co.us
Internet:
http://www.dora.state.co.us/Securities/

Connecticut Securities and Business
Investments Division
Department of Banking
260 Constitution Plaza
Hartford, Connecticut 06103-1800
Phone: (860) 240-8230
Fax: (860) 240-8295
e-mail: Mailboxes at Securities & Business
Investments Division
Internet: http://www.state.ct.us/dob/pages/
secdiv.htm

Delaware Division of Securities
Department of Justice
820 North French Street, 5th Floor
Carvel State Office Building
Wilmington, Delaware 19801
Phone: (302) 577-8424
Fax: (302) 577-6987
Internet:
http://www.state.de.us/securities/index.htm

District of Columbia Department of
Insurance and Securities Regulation
810 First Street NE, 6th Floor
Washington, D.C. 20002
Phone: (202) 727-8000
Fax: (202) 535-1199

Florida Department of
Banking & Finance
101 East Gaines Street
Plaza Level , The Capitol
Tallahassee, Florida 32399-0350
Phone: (850) 488-9805
Fax: (850) 681-2428
e-mail: dbf@mail.dbf.state.fl.us
Internet: http://www.dbf.state.fl.us/
licensing/licensingreg.html

Georgia Division of Securities
& Business Regulation
Two Martin Luther King, Jr. Drive SE
802 West Tower
Atlanta, Georgia 30334
Phone: (404)656-3920

Fax: (404)651-6451
Internet: http://www.sos.state.ga.us/
securities/default.htm

Hawaii Securities Compliance Branch
Department of Commerce
& Consumer Affairs
1010 Richards Street
Honolulu, Hawaii 96813
Mailing address:
P.O. Box 40
Honolulu, Hawaii 96810
Phone: (808) 586-2744
Fax: (808) 586-2733
Internet: http://www.state.hi.us/dcca/
breg-seu/index.html

Idaho Department of Finance
Securities Bureau
700 West State Street, 2nd Floor
Boise, Idaho 83720
Mailing Address:
P.O. Box 83720
Boise, Idaho 83720-0031
Phone: (208) 332-8004
Fax: (208) 332-8099
Internet:
http://www.state.id.us./finance/sec.htm

Illinois

Illinois Securities Department
Office of the Secretary of State
17 North State Street, Suite 1100
Chicago, Illinois 60601
Phone: (312) 793-3384 or (800) 628-7937
Fax: (312)793-1202

Springfield office:
Suite 200 Lincoln Tower
520 South Second Street
Springfield, Illinois 62701
Phone: (217) 782-8876
Fax: (217) 524-9637
Internet: http://www.sos.state.il.us/
depts/securities/sec_home.html

Indiana Securities Division
Office of the Secretary of State
302 West Washington, Room E-111
Indianapolis, Indiana 46204
Phone: (317) 232-6681
1-800-223-8791
Fax: (317) 233-3675
e-mail: Send Mail From Web Site
Internet: http://www.ai.org/sos/security/

Iowa Securities Bureau
Insurance Division
340 E. Maple
Des Moines, Iowa 50319-0066
Phone: (515) 281-4441
Fax(1): (515) 281-3059

Fax(2): (515) 281-6467
e-mail: iowasec@comm6.state.ia.us
Internet: http://www.state.ia.us/ins/security/

Kansas Office of the Securities Commissioner
618 South Kansas Avenue, 2nd Floor
Topeka, Kansas 66603-3804
Phone: (785) 296-3307 or (800) 232-9580
Fax: (785) 296-6872
e-mail: ksecom@cjnetworks.com
Internet: http://www.cjnetworks.com/~ksecom/

Wichita office:
Office of the Securities Commissioner
230 E. William, Suite 7080
Wichita, Kansas 67202
Phone: (316) 337-6280
Fax: (316) 337-6282
e-mail: kscict@feist.com

Kentucky Department of Financial
Institutions
1025 Capital Center Drive, Suite 200
Frankfort, KY 40601
Phone: (502) 573-3390 or (800) 223-2579
Fax: (502) 573-8787
e-mail: Mailboxes at KY DFI
Internet: http://www.dfi.state.ky.us/
security/Security.html

Louisiana Securities Division
Office of Financial Institutions
3445 North Causeway Blvd., Suite 509
Metairie, LA 70002
Phone: (504) 846-6970
Fax:
e-mail: la_ofi@mail.premier.net
Internet: http://www.ofi.state.la.us/securit.htm

Maine Securities Division
Bureau of Banking
Department of Professional & Financial
Regulation
121 State House Station
Augusta, Maine 04333-0121
Phone: (207) 624-8551
Fax: (207) 624-8590
e-mail: Mailboxes at ME Securities Division
Internet: http://www.state.me.us/pfr/sec/
sechome2.htm

Maryland Division of Securities
Office of the Attorney General
200 Saint Paul Place, 20th Floor
Baltimore, Maryland 21202-2020
Phone: (410) 576-6360
Fax: (410) 576-6532
e-mail: securities@oag.state.md.us
Internet: http://www.oag.state.md.us/
Securities/index.htm

Massachusetts Securities Division
Secretary of the Commonwealth
One Ashburton Place, Room 1701
Boston, Massachusetts 02108
Phone: (617) 727-3548
800-269-5428 *(in Massachusetts only)*
Fax: (617) 248-0177
e-mail: securities@sec.state.ma.us
Internet:
http://www.state.ma.us/sec/sct/sctidx.htm

Michigan Securities Bureau
Office of Financial and Insurance Services
6546 Mercantile Way
Lansing, Michigan 48908
Mailing Address:
P.O. Box 30701
Lansing, MI 48909-8201
Overnight Delivery Address:
7150 Harris Dr.
P.O. Box 30701
Lansing, MI 48909
Phone: (517) 334-6213
Fax: (517) 334-7813
E-mail: ronald.c.jones@cis.state.mi.us
Internet: http://www.cis.state.mi.us/
corp/divisions/sec_ex_div/home.htm

Minnesota Division of Securities
Department of Commerce
133 East Seventh Street
St. Paul, Minnesota 55101
Phone: (651) 296-4026
Fax: (651) 296-9434
e-mail: securities@state.mn.us
Internet: http://www.commerce.state.
mn.us/mainrg.htm

Mississippi Securities Division
Secretary of State's Office
202 North Congress Street, Suite 601
Jackson, MS 39201
Mailing address:
P.O. Box 136
Jackson, MS 39205
Phone: 1-800-804-6364
Fax: (601) 359-2894
e-mail: administrator@sos.state.ms.us
Internet: http://www.sos.state.ms.us/busserv/
securities/securities.html

Missouri Securities Division
Office of the Secretary of State
600 West Main Street
Jefferson City, MO 65101
Phone: (573) 751-4136
Fax: (573) 526-3124
Internet: http://mosl.sos.state.mo.us/
sos-sec/sossec.html

Montana Securities Division
Office of the State Auditor
126 North Sanders, Room 270

Helena, Montana 59604
Mailing address:
P.O. Box 4009
Helena, Montana 59604
Phone: (406) 444-2040
1-800-332-6148 (in-state only)
Fax: (406) 444-5558
e-mail: Mailboxes at Securities Division
Internet: http://www.state.mt.us/sao/
secdiv.htm

Nebraska Bureau of Securities
Department of Banking & Finance
1200 N Street, Suite 311
Lincoln, Nebraska 68508
Mailing address:
P.O. Box 95006
Lincoln, Nebraska 68509-5006
Phone: (402) 471-3445
Fax:
e-mail: Mailboxes at NE Securities Bureau
Internet: http://www.ndbf.org/SEC.HTM

Nevada Securities Division
Secretary of State
555 E. Washington Avenue
5th Floor, Suite 5200
Las Vegas, NV 89101
Phone: (702) 486-2440
Fax: (702) 486-2452
e-mail: nvsec@govmail.state.nv.us
Internet: http://sos.state.nv.us/securities/

Reno office:
Office of the Secretary of State
Securities Division
1105 Terminal Way, Suite 211
Reno, NV 89502
Phone: (775) 688-1855
Fax: (775) 688-1858
E-mail: securrno@govmail.state.nv.us

New Hampshire Bureau of Securities
Regulation
Department of State
State House, Annex - Room 317A
25 Capital Street
Concord, New Hampshire 03301

Mailing Address:
Room 204, State House
Concord, NH 03301-4989
Phone: (603) 271-1463
Fax: (603) 271-7933
Internet: http://www.state.nh.us/sos/

New Jersey Bureau of Securities
Department of Law & Public Safety
153 Halsey Street, 6th Floor
Newark, New Jersey 07102

Mailing Address:
P.O. Box 47029
Newark, New Jersey 07101

Phone: (973) 504-3600
Fax: (973) 504-3601
Internet:
http://www.state.nj.us/lps/ca/bos.htm

New Mexico Securities Division
Regulation & Licensing Department
725 St. Michaels Drive
Santa Fe, New Mexico 87505-7605
Phone: (505) 827-7140
Fax: (505) 984-0617
E-mail: RLDSD@state.nm.us
Internet: http://www.rld.state.nm.us/
sec/index.htm

New York Bureau of Investor Protection
& Securities
Office of Attorney General
120 Broadway, 23rd Floor
New York, New York 10271
Phone: (212) 416-8200
Fax: (212) 416-8816
e-mail: E-mail from Web site
Internet: http://www.oag.state.ny.us/
investors/investors.html

North Carolina Securities Division
Department of the Secretary of State
300 North Salisbury Street, Suite 301
Raleigh, North Carolina 27603-5909
Phone: (919) 733-3924
Fax: (919) 821-0818
Internet: http://www.secretary.state.nc.us/sec/

North Dakota Securities Commissioner
State Capitol, 5th Floor
600 E. Boulevard
Bismarck, North Dakota 58505-0510
Phone: (701) 328-2910
Fax: (701) 255-3113
e-mail: seccom@pioneer.state.nd.us
Internet: http://www.state.nd.us/
securities/

Ohio Division of Securities
77 South High Street, 22nd Floor
Columbus, Ohio 43215
Phone: (614) 644-7381
Fax: (614) 466-3316
e-mail: Mailboxes at the Division of
Securities
Internet: http://www.securities.state.oh.us

Oklahoma Department of Securities
First National Center, Suite 860
120 N. Robinson
Oklahoma City, OK 73102
Phone: (405) 280-7700
Fax: (405) 280-7742
E-mail: Mailboxes at Dept. of Securities
Internet: http://www.securities.state.ok.us/

Oregon Division of Finance and Corporate
Securities
Department of Consumer & Business Services
350 Winter Street NE, Room 410
Salem, Oregon 97310
Phone: (503) 378-4387
Fax: (503) 947-7862
e-mail: Richard.m.nockleby@state.or.us
Internet: http://www.cbs.state.or.us/exter-
nal/dfcs/

Pennsylvania Securities Commission
Eastgate Office Building
1010 North 7th Street - 2nd Floor
Harrisburg, Pennsylvania 17102-1410
Phone: (717) 787-8061
Fax: (717) 783-5122
E-mail: pscwebmaster@state.pa.us
Internet: http://www.psc.state.pa.us/
PA_Exec/Securities/

Philadelphia office:
1109 State Office Building
Philadelphia, Pennsylvania 19130-4088
Phone: (215) 560-2088
Fax: (215) 560-3977

Pittsburgh office:
806 State Office Building
Pittsburgh, Pennsylvania 15222-1210
Phone: (412) 565-5083
Fax: (412) 565-7647

Rhode Island Securities Division
Department of Business Regulation
233 Richmond Street, Suite 232
Providence, Rhode Island 02903-4232
Phone: (401) 222-3048
TDD#: (401) 222-2223
Fax: (401) 222-5629
e-mail: secdiv@dbr.state.ri.us
Internet: http://www.state.ri.us/manual/data/
queries/stdept_idc?id=19

South Carolina Securities Division
Office of the Attorney General
Rembert C. Dennis Office Building
1000 Assembly Street
Columbia, South Carolina 29201

Mailing Address:
P.O. Box 11549
Columbia, South Carolina 29211-1549
Phone: (803) 734-4731
Fax: (803) 734-0032
e-mail: agsecurities@ag.state.sc.us
Internet: http://www.scsecurities.com

South Dakota Division of Securities
Department of Commerce and Regulation
118 West Capitol Avenue
Pierre, South Dakota 57501-2017
Phone: (605) 773-4823
Fax: (605) 773-5953

e-mail: securities@state.sd.us
Internet: http://www.state.sd.us/dcr/
securities/security.htm

Tennessee Securities Division
Department of Commerce & Insurance
Davy Crockett Tower, Suite 680
500 James Robertson Parkway
Nashville, TN 37243-0575
Phone: (615) 741-2947
1-800-863-9117 (within Tennessee)
Fax: (615) 532-8375
E-mail: dci@mail.state.tn.us
Internet: http://www.state.tn.us/commerce/
securdiv.html

Texas State Securities Board
200 East 10th Street, 5th Floor
Austin, Texas 78701
Mailing address:
P.O. Box 13167
Austin, Texas 78711-3167
Phone: (512) 305-8300
Branch Office Phone Directory
Fax: (512) 305-8310
Branch Office FAX Directory
Internet: http://www.ssb.state.tx.us

Utah Division of Securities
Heber M. Wells Building
160 East 300 South, 2nd Floor
Salt Lake City, Utah 84111

Mailing address:
P.O. Box 146760
Salt Lake City, Utah 84114-6760
Phone: (801) 530-6600
Fax: (801) 530-6980
e-mail: security@br.state.ut.us
Internet: http://www.commerce.state.ut.us/
securit/index.htm

Vermont Securities Division
Department of Banking, Insurance, Securities
& Health Care Administration
89 Main Street, 2nd Floor
Montpelier, Vermont 05620
Mailing Address:
89 Main Street - Drawer 20
Montepelier, VT 05602-3101
Phone: (802) 828-3420
Fax: (802) 828-2896
Internet: http://www.state.vt.us/bis/securi.htm

Virginia Division of Securities & Retail
Franchising
State Corporation Commission
1300 East Main Street, 9th Floor
Richmond, Virginia 23219
Mailing address:
P.O. Box 1197
Richmond, Virginia 23218
Phone: (804) 371-9051

1-800-552-7945 (in Va. only)
TDD (804) 371-9206
Fax: (804) 371-9911
Internet: http://www.state.va.us/scc/
division/srf/index.htm

Washington Securities Division
Department of Financial Institutions
General Administration Building
210 11th Street
3rd Floor West, Room 300
Olympia, WA 98504-1200
Mailing address:
P.O. Box 9033
Olympia, WA 98507-9033
Phone: (360) 902-8760
Fax: (360) 586-5068
Internet: http://www.wa.gov/dfi/securities/

West Virginia Securities Division
State Auditor's Office
State Capitol Building
Building 1, Room W-100
Charleston, West Virginia 25305
Phone: (304) 558-2257
Fax: (304) 558-4211
e-mail: securities@wvauditor.com
Internet: http://www.wvauditor.com/
securities/default.htm

Wisconsin Division of Securities
Department of Financial Institutions
345 W. Washington Ave., 4th Floor
Madison, Wisconsin 53703
Mailing address:
P.O. Box 1768
Madison, Wisconsin 53701-1768
Phone: (608) 261-9555
Fax: (608) 256-1259
E-mail: askthesecretary@dfi.state.wi.us
Internet: http://www.wdfi.org/

Wyoming Securities Division
Secretary of State
State Capitol, Room 109
200 W. 24th Street
Cheyenne, Wyoming 82002-0020
Phone: (307) 777-7370
Fax: (307) 777-5339
e-mail: securities@missc.state.wy.us
Internet:
http://soswy.state.wy.us/securiti/securiti.htm

Puerto Rico Commissioner of Financial
Institutions
P.O. Box 11855
Fernandez Juncos Station
San Juan, Puerto Rico 00910-3855
Phone: (787) 723-3131
Fax: (787) 723-4225
E-mail: webmaster@cif.gov.pr
Internet: http://cif.gov.pr/html/message.html

RUNNING A CORPORATION 6

DAY-TO-DAY ACTIVITIES

There are not many differences between running a corporation and any other type of business. The most important point to remember is to keep the corporation's affairs separate from your personal affairs. The corporation should not make frequent loans to its shareholders, and funds of the corporation and individual shareholders should not be commingled. Funds taken out or put into the corporation should be documented. The decision of whether these should be salary, loans, dividends or otherwise, should be made with the help of an accountant or good tax guide based upon your financial situation.

Another important point to remember is to always refer to the corporation as a corporation. *Always* use the complete corporate name including designations such as "Inc." or "Corp." on *everything. Always* sign corporate documents with your corporate title. If you don't, you may lose your protection from liability. There have been many cases where persons forgot to put the word "pres." or "president" after their name when entering into contracts for the corporation. As a result, the persons were determined to be personally liable for performance of the contract.

CORPORATE RECORDS

MINUTE BOOK
A corporation must keep minutes of the proceedings of its shareholders, board of directors, and committees of directors. The minutes should be in writing. Some states allow minutes to be kept in forms other than writing provided they can be converted into written form within a reasonable time. This would mean that they could be kept in a computer or possibly on a videotape. However, it is always best to keep a duplicate copy or at least one written copy. Accidents can easily erase magnetic media.

RECORD OF SHAREHOLDERS
The corporation must also keep a record of its shareholders including the names and addresses, and the number, class, and series of shares owned. This can be kept at the registered office, principal place of business, or office of its stock transfer agent (if any). A transfer ledger can be found in Appendix C.

EXAMINATION OF RECORDS
Any shareholder of a corporation has the right to examine and copy the corporation's books and records after giving proper notice before the date on which he wishes to inspect and copy. The shareholder must have a good faith reason to inspect. He must describe his purpose, the records he wishes to inspect, and state how the purpose is related to the records.

The shareholder may have his attorney or agent examine the records and may receive photocopies of the records. The corporation may charge a reasonable fee for making photocopies. If the records are not in written form, the corporation must convert them to written form. Customarily, the corporation must bear the cost of converting all of the following to written form: the articles of incorporation and any amendments; bylaws and any amendments; resolutions by the board of directors creating different rights in the stock; minutes of all shareholders' meetings and records of any action taken by the shareholders without a meeting for the past three years; written communications to all shareholders generally or of any class, names and addresses of all officers and directors; and, the most recent report filed with the state corporate office. The shareholder may be required to pay for converting any other records to writing.

If the corporation refuses to allow a shareholder to examine the records, most states allow the shareholder to seek an order from the appropriate state court. In such a case the corporation would normally have to pay the shareholder's costs and attorney fees.

BALANCE SHEETS

Most states require a corporation to furnish its shareholders with financial statements including an end of the year balance sheet and yearly income and cash flow statements, unless exempted by shareholder resolution.

ANNUAL MEETINGS

Each year the corporation must hold annual meetings of the shareholders and directors. These meetings may be formal and held in a restaurant or they may be informal and held in the bedroom. A sole officer and director can hold them in his mind without verbally reciting all of the motions or taking a formal vote. The important thing is that the meetings are held and that minutes are kept, even by that one-man corporation. Regular minutes and meetings are evidence that the corporation is legitimate if the issue ever comes up in court. Minute forms for the annual meetings are included with this book. You can use them as master copies to photocopy each year. All that needs to be changed is the date, unless you actually change officers or directors or need to take some other corporate action.

ANNUAL REPORT

Most states require that each year every corporation must file an annual report. Many states make this a bi-annual requirement. Fortunately, this is a simple, often one-page, form that is sent to the corporation by the Secretary of State and may merely need to be signed. It contains such information as the federal tax identification number, officers' and directors' names and addresses, the registered agent's name and the address of the registered office. It must be signed and returned with the required fee by the date specified by the state. If it is not, then the corporation is dissolved after notice is given. Many states allow some corporate information (such as the registered office and agent) to be changed at this time without additional fees to the corporation. The corporation should be aware of this fact in order to avoid incurring needless expenses.

AMENDING CORPORATE INFORMATION 7

ARTICLES OF INCORPORATION

The Articles of Incorporation included in this book are very basic. Therefore they would not have to be amended except to change something major such as, the name of the corporation, or the number of shares of stock. If the amendment is made before any shares are issued it may be done by the incorporator or directors by filing an amendment to the articles, referred to as *Articles of Amendment*, *Certificate of Amendment*, or some similar title. This will be referred to as *Articles of Amendment* in this book. These are usually signed by the incorporators or director stating the name of the corporation, the amendment and date adopted, and a statement that it is made before the issue of any shares. If the amendment is made after shares have been issued, then the Articles of Amendment must be signed by the appropriate officers. The Articles of Amendment must contain the name of the corporation, the amendments, and the date of adoption by the shareholders. If the change affects the outstanding shares, then a statement must be included describing how the change will be effected.

The Articles of Amendment must be filed with the corporate filing division along with the appropriate filing fee. The fee for increasing the number of shares that the corporation is authorized to issue is more costly in many states than other amendments. The procedure for filing the Articles of Amendment depends upon who is doing the amending and at what point in time the amendment is adopted. For more information you should refer to your Secretary of State's office or your state's corporation laws.

BYLAWS

The shareholders may always amend the bylaws. The board of directors may amend the bylaws unless the articles of incorporation state otherwise or unless the shareholders provide that the bylaws may not be amended by the board.

The articles of incorporation may allow a bylaw that requires a greater quorum or voting requirement for shareholders, but such a requirement may not be adopted, amended, or repealed by the board of directors. A bylaw that fixes a greater quorum or voting requirement for the board of directors, and that was adopted by the shareholders, may be amended or repealed only by the shareholders. If it was adopted by the board it may be amended or repealed only by the board.

REGISTERED AGENT OR REGISTERED OFFICE

To change the registered agent or registered office, a form must be sent to the Secretary of State along with the appropriate fee. Most states provide a form for such a change. The form can be used to change both the registered agent and the registered office, or to just change one of them. If you are just changing one, such as the agent, then list the registered office as both the old address and the new address. A form for this purpose is included as Form T in Appendix C.

Checklist for Forming a Simple Corporation

✔ Decide on corporate name.

✔ Prepare and file Articles of Incorporation.

✔ Send for Federal Employer Identification Number (IRS Form SS-4).

✔ Prepare Shareholders' Agreement, if necessary.

✔ Meet with accountant to discuss capitalization and tax planning.

✔ If necessary meet with securities lawyer regarding stock sales.

✔ Obtain corporate seal and ring binder for minutes.

✔ Pay any applicable taxes for sale or issuance of stock.

✔ Hold organizational meeting:

    ✔ Complete Bylaws, Waiver, Minutes, Offers to Purchase Stock.

    ✔ Sign all documents and place in minute book.

✔ Issue stock certificates:

    ✔ Be sure consideration is paid.

    ✔ Complete Bill of Sale if property is traded for stock.

✔ File fictitious name if one will be used.

✔ Get licenses.

✔ Open bank account.

✔ For S-Corporation status file Form 2553.

Appendix A
State-by-State
Incorporation Laws

The following pages contain a listing of each state's corporation laws and fees. Because the laws are constantly being changed by state legislatures, you should call before filing your papers to confirm the fees and other requirements. The phone numbers are provided for each state.

In the continued growth of the world wide web, more and more state corporation divisions are making their fees and procedures available online. Some states have downloadable forms available and some even allow you to search their entire database from the comfort of your home or office.

The best web sites at the time of publication of this book are included for each state. However, the sites change constantly so you may need to look a little deeper if your state's site has changed its address.

ALABAMA

Title 10-2A, Alabama Statutes
  Secretary of State
  Corporation Section
  P.O. Box 5616
  Montgomery, AL 36103-5616
  Tel: (334) 242-5324
  Web site: http://www.sos.state.al.us

I.   ARTICLES OF INCORPORATION
    A. Must file the original and two exact copies of the Articles in the office of the probate judge in the county where the initial registered office of the corporation will be located.

II. THE CORPORATE NAME
    A. Name must contain the word "corporation," "incorporated," or abbreviation of the same.
    B. Prior to incorporation, a corporate name may be reserved for a period of 120 days. Name may be reserved by telephone, subject to further secretary of state requirements.
    C. There is no fee charged when initially registering the corporate name. The fee is included with the filing fee. If the name is reserved prior to filing the articles, there is no charge initially assessed. However, if the articles are not filed within 120 days, the incorporator is billed the $10.00.

III. DIRECTORS
    A. Directors need not be residents of the state or shareholders of the corporation.
    B. The articles or bylaws may prescribe additional requirements or qualifications.
    C. A corporation must have one director or more as initially stated in articles and thereafter as many directors as stated in bylaws.
    D. Director(s) are normally elected at the annual meeting of shareholders.

IV. OFFICERS
    A. A corporation must have a president and secretary. Other officers may be elected or appointed in accordance with provisions set forth in the bylaws.
    B. The same person may hold more than one office unless provided for otherwise in the bylaws.
    C. An officer performs duties stated in the bylaws or by the board of directors or another officer to the extent consistent with the bylaws.

V.   REGISTERED AGENT
    A. A corporation must register an agent for service of process with the state who has an office within the state.

VI. FILING FEES
    A. Articles of Incorporation
        1. State of Alabama $50.00
        2. County Probate Judge $35.00
    B. Application for Name Reservation $10.00 (if Articles not filed as described in IIc above)
    C. Amending Articles of Incorporation
        1. County Probate Judge $10.00
        2. State of Alabama $20.00 (for name change only)
    D. Filing Annual Report State of Alabama
        (minimum fee based on $5000 of capital stock) $10.00
    E. Cost for Certified Copy of Any Document $1.00/page plus $5.00 to certify the document

Note: The minimum filing fee to initially incorporate is $85.00 for the filing of the articles and the application for name reservation. Many banks request a certified copy of the Articles prior to setting up a corporate account. Therefore, the certification cost is often necessary as well.

ALASKA

Title 10, Alaska Statutes

Department of Community and Economic Development
Division of B.S.C.
Attention: Corporation Section
P.O. Box 110808
Juneau, AK 99811-0808
Tel: (907) 465-2530
Fax: (907) 465-3257

Web site: http://www.dced.state.ak.us/bsc/corps.htm

I.   ARTICLES OF INCORPORATION
     A.   Must provide state corporation office with the original and one exact copy of the Articles.

II. THE CORPORATE NAME
     A.   Name must contain the word "corporation," "incorporated," "company," "limited," or abbreviation of the same.
     B.   Name must not contain the word "city," "borough," or "village."
     C.   Prior to incorporation, a corporate name may be reserved for a period of 120 days.

III. DIRECTORS
     A.   Directors need not be residents of the state or shareholders of the corporation.
     B.   The articles or bylaws may prescribe additional requirements or qualifications.
     C.   A corporation must have more than one director. If the number of directors is not set, the number of directors shall be three.
     D.   Director(s) are normally elected at the annual meeting of shareholders.

IV. OFFICERS
     A.   A corporation must have a president, secretary and treasurer. Other officers may be elected or appointed in accordance with provisions set forth in the bylaws.
     B.   The same person may hold as many as two offices, except for the president and secretary. If all issued stock is owned by one person, he may hold all offices.
     C.   An officer performs duties stated in the bylaws or by the board of directors or another officer to the extent consistent with the bylaws.

V.   REGISTERED AGENT
     A.   A corporation must register an agent with the state who has an office within the state.

VI. FILING FEES
     A. Articles of Incorporation $250.00
     B. Change of Registered Agent & Acceptance $25.00
     C. Application for Name Reservation $25.00
     D. Amending Articles of Incorporation $25.00
     E. Filing Biennial Report $100.00
     F. Cost for Certified Copy of Articles $15.00

Note: The filing fees include $150.00 for the actual filing of the articles and $100.00 for the initial biennial report.

ARIZONA

Title 10, Arizona Statutes

Arizona Corporation Commission
1300 W. Washington
Phoenix, AZ 85007-2929
(602) 542-3135
(800) 345-5819 (Arizona residents only)
or
400 W. Congress
Tucson, AZ 85701-1347
(520) 628-6560

Web site: http://www.cc.state.az.us/corp/index.ssi

I.   ARTICLES OF INCORPORATION
    A.   One person must act as incorporators.
    B.   Must provide state corporation office with the original and one exact copy of the Articles. The copy will be returned to the incorporators within 60 days. It must be published for 3 consecutive publications in a newspaper of general circulation in the county of the known place of business.

II. THE CORPORATE NAME
    A.   Name must contain the word "corporation," "incorporated," "company," "limited," or abbreviation of the same.
    B.   Prior to incorporation, a corporate name may be reserved for a period of 120 days.

III. DIRECTORS
    A.   Directors need not be residents of the state or shareholders of the corporation.
    B.   The articles or bylaws may prescribe additional requirements or qualifications.
    C.   A corporation must have one director or more as initially stated in articles and thereafter as many directors as stated in bylaws.
    D.   Director(s) are normally elected at the annual meeting of shareholders.

IV. OFFICERS
    A.   A corporation must have a president, one or more vice presidents, a secretary and a treasurer. Other officers may be elected or appointed in accordance with provisions set forth in the bylaws.
    B.   The same person may hold more than one office except for the president and the secretary.
    C.   An officer performs duties stated in the bylaws or by the board of directors or another officer to the extent consistent with the bylaws.

V.   REGISTERED AGENT
    A.   Corporation must have a statutory agent at a known place of business within the state.

VI. FILING FEES
    A. Articles of Incorporation $60.00
    B. Amending Articles of Incorporation $25.00
    C. Filing Annual Report $45.00
    D. Cost for Certified Copy of Document $5.00 + .50/page (LLC = $10.00 + $.50/page)
    E. Fee for Publishing Articles or Amendments in County of Business
    F. Name Reservation $10.00
    G. Expedited filing within 3-5 business days $35.00
        Variable, depending on the newspaper and length of articles

ARKANSAS

Title 4, Chapter 27, Arkansas Statutes

Secretary of State
Corporation Division
State Capital, Room 58
Little Rock, AR 72201
(501) 682-5151

Web site: http://www.sosweb.state.ar.us

I.   ARTICLES OF INCORPORATION
   A.   Must be printed or typewritten in English.
   B.   Must provide state corporation office with duplicate originals of the Articles and a completed corporate franchise tax form.

II.   THE CORPORATE NAME
   A.   Name must indicate its corporate character. This can be done by using such words as "corporation," "incorporated," "company," "limited," or abbreviation of the same.
   B.   Prior to incorporation, a corporate name may be reserved for a period of 120 days.
   C.   Foreign corporations may do name registration.

III.   DIRECTORS
   A.   Directors need not be residents of the state or shareholders of the corporation unless bylaws require it.
   B.   The articles or bylaws may prescribe additional requirements or qualifications.
   C.   A corporation must have at least one director unless there are less than three directors. The number of directors may be increased or decreased by amending the articles or bylaws in a manner set forth in the articles or bylaws.
   D.   Director(s) are normally elected at the annual meeting of shareholders unless the terms are staggered.

IV.   OFFICERS
   A.   A corporation must have at least two different individuals as officers unless one person owns all the voting stock then the same person may hold all offices. Other officers may be elected or appointed in accordance with provisions set forth in the bylaws.
   B.   An officer performs duties stated in the bylaws or by the board of directors or another officer to the extent consistent with the bylaws.
   C.   One officer shall be responsible for preparing the records of any director or shareholder meeting.

V.   REGISTERED AGENT
   A.   A corporation must register an agent with the state who is a resident with a physical address in Arkansas; or a corporation with a business office identical with the registered office; or a foreign corporation authorized to do business in Arkansas whose business office is identical with the registered office.

VI.   FILING FEES
   A. Articles of Incorporation $50.00
   B. Change of Registered Agent' Name/Address $25.00
   C. Application for Name Reservation $25.00
   D. Amending Articles of Incorporation $50.00
   E. Filing Annual Report (Minimum) $50.00
   F. Cost for Certified Copy of Any Document $5.00 + .50/page

Note: In filing the annual franchise tax report, fee is based on value of stock.

CALIFORNIA

California Corporation Code, Title 1

Secretary of State
Corporate Division
Attn: Legal Review
1500 11th Street, 3rd floor
Sacramento, CA 95814
(916) 653-2318

Web site: http://www.ss.ca.gov/

I.   ARTICLES OF INCORPORATION
   A.   Must provide state corporation office with the original and two typed copies of the Articles.

II.   THE CORPORATE NAME
   A.   Name must contain "corporation," "incorporated," or "limited" or an abbreviation of the same.
   B.   Name must not contain words which are likely to mislead the public or contain the words "bank," "trust," "trustee" or related words.
   C.   Prior to incorporation, a corporate name may be reserved for a nonrenewable period of 60 days.

III.   DIRECTORS
   A.   Directors need not be residents of the state or shareholders of the corporation.
   B.   The articles or bylaws may prescribe additional requirements or qualifications.
   C.   A corporation must have three directors or more as initially stated in articles and thereafter as many directors as stated in bylaws. However, when there are less than three shareholders, there need be only a corresponding number of directors.
   D.   Director(s) are normally elected at the annual meeting of shareholders.

IV.   OFFICERS
   A.   A corporation must have a president and/or a chairman of the board, a secretary and a chief financial officer. Other officers may be elected or appointed in accordance with provisions set forth in the bylaws.
   B.   The same person may hold more than one office unless provided for otherwise in the bylaws.
   C.   An officer performs duties stated in the bylaws or by the board of directors or another officer to the extent consistent with the bylaws.

V.   REGISTERED AGENT
   A.   A corporation must register an agent with the state who has an office within the state.

VI.   FILING FEES
   A. Articles of Incorporation $100.00
   B. Change of Registered Agent & Acceptance $5.00
   C. Application for Name Reservation $10.00
   D. Amending Articles of Incorporation $30.00
   E. Filing Annual Report $20.00
   F. Cost for Certified Copy of Any Document $8.00
   G. Minimum annual franchise tax   *$800.00
   H. Expedited filing $15.00

* Must be paid when Articles are filed, for a total of $900.00 to incorporate.

Colorado

Title 7, Colorado Revised Statutes

Secretary of State
Corporations Office
1560 Broadway, Suite 200
Denver, CO 80202
Tel: (303) 894-2251
Fax:(303) 894-2242

Web site:http://www.sos.state.co.us

I.   ARTICLES OF INCORPORATION
   A.   Must provide state corporation office with two sets of original Articles, typed.
   B.   Must record certificate of incorporation in each county where the corporation owns real property.

II. THE CORPORATE NAME
   A.   Name must contain the word "corporation," "incorporated," "company" or "limited," or abbreviation of the same.
   B.   Prior to incorporation, a corporate name may be reserved for a period of 120 days and is renewable for another 120 days. Name may not be reserved by telephone, although a name search can be done by this method. A name search for up to 3 names can be done by fax for $3.00. Allow 2-3 business days for a response.

III. DIRECTORS
   A.   Director(s) must be at least 18 years of age but need not be a resident of the state or a shareholder of the corporation.
   B.   The articles or bylaws may prescribe additional requirements or qualifications.
   C.   A corporation must have three directors or more as initially stated in articles and thereafter as many directors as stated in bylaws. However, when there are less than three shareholders, there need be only a corresponding number of directors.
   D.   Director(s) are normally elected at the annual meeting of shareholders.

IV. OFFICERS
   A.   A corporation must have a president, secretary and treasurer who are elected by the board and must be at least 18 years of age. Other officers may be elected or appointed in accordance with provisions set forth in the bylaws.
   B.   The same person may hold more than one office except the offices of president and secretary and unless prohibited from doing so in the bylaws.
   C.   An officer performs duties stated in the bylaws or by the board of directors to the extent consistent with the bylaws.

V.   REGISTERED AGENT
   A.   A corporation must register an agent with the state who has an office within the state.

VI. FILING FEES
   A. Articles of Incorporation $50.00
   B. Change of Registered Agent & Acceptance $ 5.00
   C. Application for Name Reservation $10.00
   D. Amending Articles of Incorporation $25.00
   E. Filing Annual Report $25.00
   F. Cost for Certified Copy of Any Document $2.00 + $.50 per page

CONNECTICUT

Chapter 601, Business Corporations—Connecticut Business Corporation Act

Secretary of State
30 Trinity Street
P.O. Box 150470
Hartford, CT 06106-0470
(860) 509-6003 (Document Review)

Web site: http://www.sots.state.ct.us

I.   CERTIFICATE OF INCORPORATION
   A. Must be printed or typewritten in English.
   B. Must provide state corporation office with the original and one exact copy of the Certificate.

II. THE CORPORATE NAME
   A. Name must contain the word "corporation," "incorporated," "company," "limited," or abbreviation of the same.
   B. Prior to incorporation, a corporate name may be reserved for a period of 120 days.

III. DIRECTORS
   A. Directors need not be residents of the state or shareholders of the corporation.
   B. The certificate or bylaws may prescribe additional requirements or qualifications.
   C. A corporation must have three directors or more as initially stated in articles and thereafter as many directors as stated in bylaws. However, when there are less than three shareholders, there need be only a corresponding number of directors.
   D. Director(s) are normally elected at the annual meeting of shareholders.

IV. OFFICERS
   A. A corporation must have a president and secretary. Other officers may be elected or appointed in accordance with provisions set forth in the bylaws.
   B. The same person may hold more than one office except for the offices of president and secretary.
   C. An officer performs duties stated in the bylaws or by the board of directors to the extent consistent with the bylaws.

V.   REGISTERED AGENT
   A. Corporation must register with the state an agent at an office within the state.

VI. FILING FEES for DOMESTIC STOCK CORPORATIONS
   A. Certificate of Incorporation $50.00
   B. Change of Registered Agent & Acceptance $25.00
   C. Application for Name Reservation $30.00
   D. Amending Certificate of Incorporation $50.00
   E. Filing Reports
      1. Annual report $75.00
      2. Biennial report $150.00
      3. Corrected report $50.00
   F. Cost for Certified Copy of Any Document $25.00
   G. Franchise tax for stock corporation $150.00 minimum
   Tax rate: One cent per share for the first 10,000 shares; plus 1/2 cent per share for the first 10,001-100,000 shares; plus 1/4 cent per share for 100,001-1,000,000 shares; plus 1/5 cent per share for each share in excess of 1,000,000.
   H. Expedited filing available $25.00

Note: The minimum fee for initial incorporation is $325.00 for the filing fee, organizational tax and initial biennial report.

DELAWARE

Title 8, Delaware Code

Secretary of State
Division of Corporations
401 Federal St. #4
Dover, DE 19901
(302) 739-3073

Web site: http://www.state.de.us/corp

I. CERTIFICATE OF INCORPORATION
    A. Must be printed or typewritten in English.
    B. Must provide state corporation office with the original and one exact copy of the Certificate.
    C. Must record a copy of the Certificate in the county where the registered office is located.

II. THE CORPORATE NAME
    A. Name must contain the word "corporation," "incorporated," "association," "company," "club," "foundation," "fund," "institute," "society," "union," "syndicate" or "limited," or abbreviation of the same.
    B. Prior to incorporation, a corporate name may be reserved for a period of 30 days. Name may be reserved by telephone by calling (900) 420-8042.

III. DIRECTORS
    A. Directors need not be residents of the state or shareholders of the corporation.
    B. The articles or bylaws may prescribe additional requirements or qualifications.
    C. A corporation must have one director or more as initially stated in articles and thereafter as many directors as stated in bylaws.
    D. Director(s) are normally elected at the annual meeting of shareholders.

IV. OFFICERS
    A. A corporation may have officers which are elected or appointed in accordance with provisions set forth in the bylaws or determined by the directors.
    B. The same person may hold more than one office unless provided for otherwise in the bylaws.
    C. An officer performs duties stated in the bylaws or by the board of directors or another officer to the extent consistent with the bylaws.
    D. One officer shall be responsible for preparing the records of any director or shareholder meeting.

V. REGISTERED AGENT
    A. A corporation must register an agent with the state who has an office within the state.

VI. FILING FEES
    A. Receiving & Indexing Certificate of Incorporation $50.00
    B. Application for Name Reservation   N/C
    C. Amending Articles of Incorporation $100.00 (includes filing fee, receiving & indexing)
    D. Filing Annual Report $20.00
    E. Cost for Certified Copy of Any Document $20.00 + $1.00 per page
    F. Incorporation Tax (for up to 1500 shares) $15.00
    G. Expedited services
       24 hours   up to $100.00
       same day   up to $200.00
       2 hours $500.00

Note: The minimum filing fee to initially incorporate is $50.00 for the receiving and indexing of the Certificate of Incorporation, the Incorporation Tax and one Certified Copy.

DISTRICT OF COLUMBIA

Title 29, District of Columbia Code

Department of Consumer and Regulatory Affairs
Corporation Division
941 N. Capitol St. N.E.
Washington, D.C. 20002
(202) 442-4400

Web site: http://www.dcra.org/formlist.htm

I. ARTICLES OF INCORPORATION
    A. Must be printed or typewritten in English.
    B. Must provide Department of Consumer and Regulatory Affairs with duplicate originals.

II. THE CORPORATE NAME
    A. Name must contain the word "corporation," "incorporated," "company," or "limited," or abbreviation of the same.
    B. Prior to incorporation, a corporate name may be reserved for a period of 60 days.

III. DIRECTORS
    A. Directors need not be a shareholder of the corporation.
    B. The articles or bylaws may prescribe additional requirements or qualifications.
    C. A corporation must have three directors or more as initially stated in articles and thereafter as many directors as stated in bylaws.
    D. Director(s) are normally elected at the annual meeting of shareholders.

IV. OFFICERS
    A. A corporation must have a president, one or more vice presidents, secretary and treasurer. Other officers may be elected or appointed in accordance with provisions set forth in the bylaws.
    B. The same person may hold more than one office except of president and secretary unless prohibited from doing so in the bylaws.
    C. An officer performs duties stated in the bylaws or by the board of directors or another officer to the extent consistent with the bylaws.

V. REGISTERED AGENT
    A. A corporation must register an agent with the state who has an office within the district.

VI. FILING FEES
    A. Articles of Incorporation $100.00
    B. Designation of Registered Agent & Acceptance $25.00
    C. Application for Name Reservation $25.00
    D. Amending Articles of Incorporation* $100.00
    E. Filing Biennial Report $200.00
    F. Cost for Certified Copy of Any Document $5.00

* Except for changes in numbers of shares

FLORIDA

Chapters 607 and 621, Florida Statutes

> Secretary of State
> Division of Corporations
> P.O. Box 6327
> Tallahassee, FL 32314
> Street address: 409 E. Gaines St.
> Tallahassee, FL 32399
> (904) 488-9000
> (904) 487-6052

> Web site: http://www.dos.state.fl.us

I. ARTICLES OF INCORPORATION
    A. Must be printed or typewritten in English.
    B. Must provide state corporation office with the original and one exact copy of the Articles.

II. THE CORPORATE NAME
    A. Name must contain the word "corporation," "incorporated," "company," or abbreviation of the same.
    B. Prior to incorporation, a corporate name may be reserved for a non-renewable period of 120 days.

III. DIRECTORS
    A. Director(s) must be a natural person, 18 years of age, but need not be a resident of the state or a shareholder of the corporation.
    B. The articles or bylaws may prescribe additional requirements or qualifications.
    C. A corporation must have one director or more as initially stated in articles and thereafter as many directors as stated in bylaws.
    D. Director(s) are normally elected at the annual meeting of shareholders.

IV. OFFICERS
    A. A corporation must have the officers described in its bylaws or appointed in accordance with provisions set forth in the bylaws.
    B. The same person may hold more than one office unless provided for otherwise in the bylaws.
    C. An officer performs duties stated in the bylaws or by the board of directors or another officer to the extent consistent with the bylaws.
    D. One officer shall be responsible for preparing the records of any director or shareholder meeting.

V. REGISTERED AGENT
    A. A corporation must register an agent with the state who has an office within the state.

VI. FILING FEES
    A. Articles of Incorporation $35.00
    B. Designation of Registered Agent & Acceptance $35.00
    C. Application for Name Reservation $35.00
    D. Amending Articles of Incorporation $35.00
    E. Filing Annual Report $150.00 if received before May 1
                                                        $550.00 if received after May 1
    F. Cost for Certified Copy of Any Document $8.75 (plus $1 per page for each page over 8, not to exceed a maximum of $52.50)

Note: The minimum filing fee is $70 to initially incorporate includes the filing of the Articles of Incorporation and Designation of Registered Agent.

GEORGIA

Title 14, Georgia Code

Secretary of State
315 West Tower
#2 Martin Luther King, Jr. Drive
Atlanta, GA 30334-1530
Tel: (404) 656-2817
Fax:(404) 651-9059

Web site: http://www.SOS.State.Ga.US/

Email: corporations@sos.state.ga.us

I.   ARTICLES OF INCORPORATION
  A. Must be printed or typewritten in English, although name of corporation may be in another language.
  B. Must provide state corporation office with the original and one exact copy of the Articles and transmittal Form 227 (see attached).
  C. Must publish notice of intent to incorporate pursuant to Georgia law.

II. THE CORPORATE NAME
  A. Name must contain the word "corporation," "incorporated," "company," "limited," or abbreviation of the same.
  B.   Prior to incorporation, a corporate name should be reserved for a nonrenewable period of 90 days. This may be done on the above web site or by calling (404) 656-2817.

III. DIRECTORS
  A. Directors must be at least 18 years of age but need not be a resident of the state or a shareholder of the corporation.
  B. The articles or bylaws may prescribe additional requirements or qualifications.
  C. A corporation must have one director or more as initially stated in articles and thereafter as many directors as stated in bylaws.
  D.   Director(s) are normally elected at the annual meeting of shareholders.

IV. OFFICERS
  A. A corporation must have the officers elected or appointed in accordance with provisions set forth in the bylaws.
  B. The same person may hold more than one office unless provided for otherwise in the bylaws.
  C. An officer performs duties stated in the bylaws or by the board of directors or another officer to the extent consistent with the bylaws.
  D. One officer shall be responsible for preparing the records of any director or shareholder meeting.

V. REGISTERED AGENT
  A. A corporation must register an agent with the state who has an office within the state.

VI. FILING FEES
A. Articles of Incorporation	$60.00
B. Application for Name Reservation	no fee
C. Amending Articles of Incorporation	$20.00
D. Filing Annual Report	$15.00
E. Fee for Publishing Notice of Intent to Incorporate	$40.00

Note: The fee for initially incorporating is $100.00 This includes filing the articles of incorporation and publishing the notice of intent to incorporate.

CATHY COX
Secretary of State

OFFICE OF SECRETARY OF STATE
CORPORATIONS DIVISION
315 West Tower, #2 Martin Luther King, Jr. Drive
Atlanta, Georgia 30334-1530
(404) 656-2817
Registered agent, officer, entity status information via the Internet
http://www.sos.state.ga.us/corporations

WARREN RARY
Director

QUINTILIS B. ROBINSON
Deputy Director

TRANSMITTAL INFORMATION
GEORGIA PROFIT OR NONPROFIT CORPORATIONS

DO NOT WRITE IN SHADED AREA - SOS USE ONLY

DOCKET #		PENDING #		CONTROL #	
DOCKET CODE	DATE FILED		AMOUNT RECEIVED		CHECK/ RECEIPT #
TYPE CODE	EXAMINER		JURISDICTION (COUNTY) CODE		

NOTICE TO APPLICANT: PRINT PLAINLY OR TYPE REMAINDER OF THIS FORM

1.

Corporate Name Reservation Number

Corporate Name

2.

Applicant/Attorney   Telephone Number

Address

City   State   Zip Code

3.

Mail or deliver to the Secretary of State, at the above address, the following:

1) This transmittal form
2) Original and one copy of the Articles of Incorporation
3) Filing fee of $60.00 payable to Secretary of State. Filing fees are NON-refundable.

I certify that a Notice of Incorporation or Notice of Intent to Incorporate with a publication fee of $40.00 has been or will be mailed or delivered to the official organ of the county where the initial registered office of the corporation is to be located. (The Clerk of Superior Court can advise you of the official organ in a particular county.)

Authorized Signature   Date

Business entity information via the Internet: http://www.sos.state.ga.us/corporations/

FORM 227

INSTRUCTIONS FOR COMPLETING FORM 227

This form must be filed with all **new** Georgia profit and nonprofit corporations. Do not file this form to change the name of an existing corporation. The form must be typed or printed in English. The form will be scanned and microfilmed, so please use black or blue ink. Articles of incorporation must be filed in addition to this form. All areas of the form must be completed or the articles of incorporation will be rejected.

1. **Corporate name reservation number. A reservation number may be obtained via the Internet,** http://www.sos.state.ga.us/corporations/request.htm. **A number may also be obtained by calling our Customer Service Group at (404) 656-2817. List the name on this form <u>exactly</u> as it appears in the articles of incorporation.**
2. **Applicant/Attorney. Provide the name and address of the applicant or filing attorney. The certificate of incorporation (or deficiency notice if the filing is incomplete) will be mailed to this address.**
3. **Signature. The applicant or filing attorney must sign and date the form. The signature certifies that the Notice of Incorporation or the Notice of Intent to Incorporate, and fee, has been or will be delivered to the appropriate publisher in accordance with Title 14 of the Official Code of Georgia Annotated. The Clerk of Superior Court can advise you regarding the appropriate publisher in a particular county.**

NOTICE TO CUSTOMERS WHO ARE CHANGING THE NAME OF A CORPORATION:

This transmittal form is not filed to change a corporate name. Articles of amendment should be filed to change the name, along with a $20.00 filing fee. The filing fee for establishing a new corporation is $60.00. The fee to change the name of an existing corporation is $20.

Please call our Customer Service Group at (404) 656-2817 with any questions, or visit our web site.

Georgia law regarding the filing of corporations may be accessed at the Secretary of State's web site, http://www.sos.state.ga.us. Click on "Corporations Division," then "Georgia Code Online." The Georgia Business Corporation Code begins at code section 14-2-101. The Georgia Nonprofit Corporation Code begins at code section 14-3-101.

Hawaii

Title 23, Hawaii Revised Statutes

> Business Registration Division
> Department of Commerce and Consumer Affairs
> 1010 Richards Street
> Honolulu, HI 96813
> (808) 586-2850

> Web site: http://www.state.hi.us/dcca/breg-seu/index.html

I. ARTICLES OF INCORPORATION
   A. Must provide state corporation office with the original Articles.
   B. All signatures must be in black ink.

II. THE CORPORATE NAME
   A. Name must contain the word "corporation," "incorporated," "limited," or abbreviation of the same.
   B. Prior to incorporation, a corporate name may be reserved for a period of 120 days. Name may be reserved by written application only.

III. DIRECTORS
   A. At least one member of the board of directors must be a resident of the state.
   B. The articles or bylaws may prescribe additional requirements or qualifications.
   C. A corporation must have three directors or more as initially stated in articles and thereafter as many directors as stated in bylaws. However, if the corporation has less than three shareholders, then only a corresponding number of directors is required.
   D. Director(s) are normally elected at the annual meeting of shareholders.

IV. OFFICERS
   A. A corporation must have a president, one or more vice presidents, a secretary and a treasurer. Other officers may be elected or appointed in accordance with provisions set forth in the bylaws.
   B. The same person may hold more than one office, including that of president and secretary, unless provided for otherwise in the bylaws. However, if the corporation has two or more directors, it must have two or more officers.
   C. An officer performs duties stated in the bylaws or by the board of directors or another officer to the extent consistent with the bylaws.

V. FILING FEES
   A. Articles of Incorporation $100.00
   B. Application for Name Reservation $20.00
   C. Amending Articles of Incorporation $50.00
   D. Filing Annual Report $25.00
   E. Cost for Certified Copy of Any Document $10.00/document plus .25/page for copying.
   F. Expedited Services $50.00

IDAHO

Title 30, Idaho Code

Secretary of State
700 W. Jefferson, Basement West
Boise, ID 83720-0080
(208) 334-2301

Web site: http://www.idsos.state.id.us/

I. ARTICLES OF INCORPORATION
   A. Must provide state corporation office with duplicate originals.

II. THE CORPORATE NAME
   A. Name must contain the word "corporation," "incorporated," "company," "limited," or abbreviation of the same.
   B. Prior to incorporation, a corporate name may be reserved for a period of four months.

III. DIRECTORS
   A. Directors need not be residents of the state or shareholders of the corporation.
   B. The articles or bylaws may prescribe additional requirements or qualifications.
   C. A corporation must have one director or more as initially stated in articles and thereafter as many directors as stated in bylaws.
   D. Director(s) are normally elected at the annual meeting of shareholders.

IV. OFFICERS
   A. A corporation must have a president, one or more vice presidents, a secretary and a treasurer. Other officers may be elected or appointed in accordance with provisions set forth in the bylaws.
   B. The same person may hold more than one office except same person cannot hold both president and secretary positions.
   C. An officer performs duties stated in the bylaws or by the board of directors or another officer to the extent consistent with the bylaws.

V. REGISTERED AGENT
   A. A corporation must register an agent with the state who has an office within the state.

VI. FILING FEES
   A. Articles of Incorporation
      • if typed (with no attachments) $100.00
      • if not typed (or with attachments) $120.00
   B. Change of Registered Agent's Name/Address $20.00
   C. Application for Name Reservation $20.00
   D. Amending Articles of Incorporation $30.00
   E. Filing Annual Report   no fee
   F. Copies $.25
      • Certification $10.00

ILLINOIS

The Business Corporation Act

> Secretary of State
> Business Services Dept.
> 328 Howlett Building
> Springfield, IL 62756
> (217) 782-6961 - forms
> (217) 782-7880 - info - Springfield
> (312) 793-3380 - info - Chicago
>
> Web site: http://www.sos.state.il.us

I.   ARTICLES OF INCORPORATION
  A.   Must provide state corporation office with duplicate originals of the Articles typewritten, black ink or computer generated.

II. THE CORPORATE NAME
  A.   Name must contain the word "corporation," "incorporated," "company" or "limited," or abbreviation of the same.
  B.   Prior to incorporation, a corporate name may be reserved for a period of 90 days. Informal requests to check name availability will be answered by telephone.

III. DIRECTORS
  A.   Directors need not be residents of the state or shareholders of the corporation.
  B.   The articles or bylaws may prescribe additional requirements or qualifications.
  C.   A corporation must have one director or more as initially stated in articles and thereafter as many directors as stated in bylaws.
  D.   Director(s) are normally elected at the annual meeting of shareholders.

IV. OFFICERS
  A.   A corporation must have the officers elected or appointed in accordance with provisions set forth in the bylaws.
  B.   The same person may hold more than one office unless provided for otherwise in the bylaws.
  C.   An officer performs duties stated in the bylaws or by the board of directors or another officer to the extent consistent with the bylaws.
  D.   One officer shall be responsible for preparing the records of any director or shareholder meeting.

V.   REGISTERED AGENT
  A.   A corporation must register an agent with the state who has an office within the state.

VI. FILING FEES

A. Articles of Incorporation (includes $25 franchise tax)	$100.00
B. Designation of Registered Agent & Acceptance	$5.00
C. Application for Name Reservation	$25.00
D. Amending Articles of Incorporation	$25.00
E. Filing Annual Report	$15.00 + fee based on capital
F. Expedited Services Available	$25.00 - $100.00

Note: The initial franchise tax is assessed at the rate of $1.50/$1,000 on the paid-in capital represented in Illinois, with a minimum tax of $25.00. Therefore, for paid-in capital up to $16,667.00, the minimum fee for initial incorporation is $100.00.

Note: All payments must be made by certified check, cashier's check, money order, Illinois' attorney's check or registered public accountant's check.

INDIANA

Title 23, Indiana Statutes

Secretary of State
Room 155, State House
302 W. Washington, Room E018
Indianapolis, IN 46204
(317) 232-6576 or
(317) 232-6531 or
(800) 726-8000

Web site: http://www.state.in.us/sos

I. ARTICLES OF INCORPORATION
  A. Must be printed or typewritten in English.
  B. Must provide state corporation office with the original and one exact copy of the Articles.

II. THE CORPORATE NAME
  A. Name must contain the word "corporation," "incorporated," "company," "limited," or abbreviation of the same.
  B. Prior to incorporation, a corporate name may be reserved for a period of 120 days. Name may be reserved only by written application.

III. DIRECTORS
  A. Directors need not be residents of the state or shareholders of the corporation.
  B. The articles or bylaws may prescribe additional requirements or qualifications.
  C. A corporation must have one director or more as initially stated in articles and thereafter as many directors as stated in bylaws.
  D. Director(s) are normally elected at the annual meeting of shareholders.

IV. OFFICERS
  A. A corporation must have the officers described in its bylaws or appointed in accordance with provisions set forth in the bylaws.
  B. The same person may hold more than one office unless provided for otherwise in the bylaws.
  C. An officer performs duties stated in the bylaws or by the board of directors or another officer to the extent consistent with the bylaws.
  D. One officer shall be responsible for preparing the records of any director or shareholder meeting.

V. REGISTERED AGENT
  A. A corporation must register an agent with the state who has an office within the state.

VI. FILING FEES
  A. Articles of Incorporation $90.00
  B. Change of Registered Agent's Name/Address $30.00
  C. Application for Name Reservation $30.00
  D. Amending Articles of Incorporation $30.00
  E. Filing Annual Report $15.00
  F. Cost for Certified Copy of Any Document $15.00/stamp plus 1.00/page

Iowa

Chapter 490, Iowa Code

> Secretary of State
> Corporations Division
> Hoover Building
> Des Moines, IA 50319
> Tel: (515) 281-5204
> Fax: (515) 242-6556
>
> Web site: http://www.sos.state.ia.us/

I. ARTICLES OF INCORPORATION
    A. Must be printed or typewritten in English.
    B. Must provide state corporation office with the original and one exact copy of the Articles.

II. THE CORPORATE NAME
    A. Name must contain the word "corporation," "incorporated," "company," "limited," or abbreviation of the same.
    B. Prior to incorporation, a corporate name may be reserved for a period of 120 days. Name may be reserved only by written application.

III. DIRECTORS
    A. Directors need not be residents of the state or shareholders of the corporation.
    B. The articles or bylaws may prescribe additional requirements or qualifications.
    C. A corporation must have one director or more as initially stated in articles and thereafter as many directors as stated in bylaws.
    D. Director(s) are normally elected at the annual meeting of shareholders.

IV. OFFICERS
    A. A corporation must have the officers elected or appointed in accordance with provisions set forth in the bylaws.
    B. The same person may hold more than one office unless provided for otherwise in the bylaws.
    C. An officer performs duties stated in the bylaws or by the board of directors or another officer to the extent consistent with the bylaws.
    D. One officer shall be responsible for preparing the records of any director or shareholder meeting.

V. REGISTERED AGENT
    A. A corporation must register an agent with the state who has an office within the state.

VI. FILING FEES
    A. Articles of Incorporation $50.00
    B. Change Registered Agent's Name/Address   no fee
    C. Application for Name Reservation $10.00
    D. Amending Articles of Incorporation $50.00
    E. Filing Biennial Report $45.00
    F. Cost for Certified Copy of Any Document $5.00/certification and 1.00/page

Kansas

Chapter 17, Kansas Statutes

> Secretary of State
> Capital Building, 2nd Floor
> 300 SW 10th St.
> Topeka, KS 66612-1594
> (785) 296-4564

Web site: http://www.state.ks.us/public/sos/

Email: kssos@kssos.org

I. ARTICLES OF INCORPORATION
    A. Must provide state corporation office with the original and a duplicate copy of the Articles.

II. THE CORPORATE NAME
    A. Name must contain the word "corporation," "incorporated," "association," "church," "college," "company," "foundation," "club," "fund," "institute," "society," "syndicate," "limited," "union," or abbreviation of the same.
    B. Prior to incorporation, a corporate name may be reserved for a period of 120 days.

III. DIRECTORS
    A. Directors need not be residents of the state or shareholders of the corporation.
    B. The articles or bylaws may prescribe additional requirements or qualifications.
    C. A corporation must have one director or more as initially stated in articles and thereafter as many directors as stated in bylaws.
    D. Director(s) are normally elected at the annual meeting of shareholders.

IV. OFFICERS
    A. A corporation must have the officers elected or appointed in accordance with provisions set forth in the bylaws.
    B. The same person may hold more than one office unless provided for otherwise in the bylaws.
    C. An officer performs duties stated in the bylaws or by the board of directors to the extent consistent with the bylaws.
    D. One officer shall be responsible for preparing the records of any director or shareholder meeting.

V. RESIDENT (REGISTERED) AGENT
    A. Corporation must register with the state a registered office and a resident agent at an office within the state.

VI. FILING FEES
A. Articles of Incorporation	$75.00
B. Application for Name Reservation	$20.00
C. Amending Articles of Incorporation (including Designation of Resident Agent)	$20.00
D. Filing Annual Report (Minimum-Maximum, depending on assets)	$20.00-2,500.00
F. Cost for Certified Copy of Any Document	$7.50 + 1.00/page

KENTUCKY

Chapter 271B, Kentucky Revised Statutes

Office of Secretary of State
P.O. Box 718
Frankfort, KY 40602-0718
(502) 564-2848, press 2 for Business filings
(502) 564-7330, press 1 for Business filings
(502) 564-4075 fax

Web site: http://www.sos.state.ky.us

I. ARTICLES OF INCORPORATION
    A. Must be printed or typewritten in English.
    B. Must provide state corporation office with the original and two exact copies of the Articles. After filing, one of the exact copies shall then be filed with and recorded by the county clerk of the county in which the registered office of the corporation is located.

II. THE CORPORATE NAME
    A. Name must contain the word "corporation," "incorporated," "company," "limited," or abbreviation of the same.
    B. Prior to incorporation, a corporate name may be reserved for a period of 120 days. A name may only be reserved in writing.

III. DIRECTORS
    A. Directors need not be residents of the state or shareholders of the corporation.
    B. The articles or bylaws may prescribe additional requirements or qualifications.
    C. A corporation must have one director or more as initially stated in articles or bylaws and thereafter as many directors as stated in bylaws.
    D. Director(s) are normally elected at the annual meeting of shareholders.

IV. OFFICERS
    A. A corporation shall have the officers described in the bylaws or appointed by the board of directors in accordance with provisions set forth in the bylaws.
    B. The same person may hold more than one office unless provided for otherwise in the bylaws.
    C. An officer performs duties stated in the bylaws or by the board of directors or another officer to the extent consistent with the bylaws.
    D. One officer shall be responsible for preparing the records of any director or shareholder meeting.

V. REGISTERED AGENT
    A. A corporation must register an agent with the state who has an office within the state.

VI. FILING FEES
A. Articles of Incorporation	$40.00
B. Change Registered Agent's Name/Address	$10.00
C. Application for Name Reservation	$15.00
D. Amending Articles of Incorporation	$40.00
E. Filing Annual Report	$15.00
F. Organizational Tax (1000 shares or less)	$10.00
G. Cost for Certified Copy of Any Document	$5.00/certificate + .50/page

Note: The minimum filing fee to initially incorporate is $50.00 which includes filing the articles of incorporation and the organizational tax for 1,000 shares or less.

LOUISIANA

Title 12, Louisiana Revised Statutes

Secretary of State
Corporations Division
P.O. Box 94125
Baton Rouge, LA 70804-9125
(225) 925-4704

Web site: http://www.sec.state.la.us/

I. ARTICLES OF INCORPORATION
A. Must be printed or typewritten in English.
B. Must provide state corporation office with the original or multiple originals of the Articles.
C. An initial report must be filed with the Articles setting forth: 1. The name and municipal address, if any, of the corporation's registered office. 2. The full name and municipal address, if any, of each of its registered agents. 3. The names and municipal addresses, if any, of its first director(s).

II. THE CORPORATE NAME
A. Name must contain the word "corporation," "incorporated," "limited," "company," or abbreviation of the same. If "company" or "co." are used, it may not be preceded by the word "and" or "&".
B. Prior to incorporation, a corporate name may be reserved for a period of 60 days. Name may be reserved only by written application.

III. DIRECTORS
A. Directors need not be residents of the state or shareholders of the corporation.
B. The articles or bylaws may prescribe additional requirements or qualifications.
C. A corporation must have three directors or more as initially stated in articles and thereafter as many directors as stated in bylaws. However, if there are less than three shareholders, there need only be as many directors as there are shareholders.
D. Director(s) are normally elected at the annual meeting of shareholders.

IV. OFFICERS
A. The board of directors of a corporation shall elect a president, secretary, treasurer and may elect one or more vice presidents. Other officers may be elected or appointed in accordance with provisions set forth in the bylaws.
B. The same person may hold more than one office unless provided for otherwise in the articles.
C. An officer performs duties stated in the bylaws or by the board of directors.

V. REGISTERED AGENT
A. A corporation must register an agent with the state who has an office within the state.

VI. FILING FEES
A. Articles of Incorporation	$60.00
B. Change of Registered Agent's Name/Address	$20.00
C. Application for Name Reservation	$20.00
D. Amending Articles of Incorporation	$60.00
E. Filing Annual Report	$25.00
F. Cost for Additional Certified Copy of Any Document	$10.00

Note: The registered agent may be changed when filing the annual report without paying the $20.00 fee.

MAINE

Title 13-A Maine Revised Statutes

Secretary of State
Bureau of Corporations, Elections, and
Commissions
101 State House Station
Augusta, ME 04333-0101
    (207) 287-4195 - forms
    (800) 872-3838 - Business Answers in Maine only
    (800) 541-5872 (outside of Maine)
Fax: (207) 287-5874

Web site: http://www.state.me.us/sos/sos.htm

I. ARTICLES OF INCORPORATION
    A. Must provide state corporation office with the original Articles.

II. THE CORPORATE NAME
    A. Name need not contain such words as "corporation," "incorporated," "company," or abbreviation of the same.
    B. Prior to incorporation, a corporate name may be reserved for a period of 120 days.

III. DIRECTORS
    A. A corporation need not have directors.
    B. Directors need not be residents of the state or shareholders of the corporation.
    C. The articles or bylaws may prescribe additional requirements or qualifications.
    D. Director(s) are normally elected at the annual meeting of shareholders.

IV. OFFICERS
    A. A corporation must have a president, treasurer and clerk. Other officers may be elected or appointed by the board of directors.
    B. The same person may hold more than one office unless provided for otherwise in the bylaws.
    C. An officer performs duties stated in the bylaws or by the board of directors or another officer to the extent consistent with the bylaws.
    D. The clerk shall be responsible for preparing the records of any director or shareholder meeting.

V. REGISTERED CLERK AND OFFICE
    A. Corporation must register with the state a clerk, who is a natural person at an office within the state.

VI. FILING FEES
    A. Articles of Incorporation $75.00
    B. Change of Registered Clerk & Acceptance $20.00
    C. Application for Name Reservation $20.00
    D. Amending Articles of Incorporation $35.00
    E. Filing Annual Report $60.00
    F. Cost for Certified Copy of Any Document $5.00 + $2.00/page
    G. Fee on authorized shares (based on amount of stock-maximum of 3000 no par or $100,000 par) $30.00

Note: The minimum filing fee to initially incorporate is $105.00 which includes the filing of the articles of incorporation and the fee on authorized shares.

MARYLAND

Corporations & Associations, Title 2, Code of Maryland

State Department of Assessments and Taxation
Charter Division
301 West Preston Street, Rm. 801
Baltimore, MD 21201
(410) 767-1350
Fax: (410) 333-7097
(800) 246-5941 (in Maryland)

Web site: http://www.sos.state.md.us/

I. ARTICLES OF INCORPORATION
    A. Must provide state corporation office with the original of the Articles, typed.

II. THE CORPORATE NAME
    A. Name must contain the word "corporation," "incorporated," "company," "limited," or abbreviation of the same.
    B. Prior to incorporation, a corporate name may be reserved by written request for a period of 30 days. Name may be checked for availability by telephone at the Department of Assessments and Taxation. If several names are being checked, the request should be made in writing.

III. DIRECTORS
    A. Directors need not be residents of the state or shareholders of the corporation.
    B. The articles or bylaws may prescribe additional requirements or qualifications.
    C. A corporation must have three directors unless no stock is outstanding or there are less than three stockholders.
    D. Director(s) are normally elected at the annual meeting of shareholders.

IV. OFFICERS
    A. A corporation must have a president, secretary and treasurer. Other officers may be elected or appointed in accordance with provisions set forth in the bylaws.
    B. The same person may hold more than one office unless provided for otherwise in the bylaws. However, the same person may not serve as both president and vice president.
    C. An officer performs duties stated in the bylaws or by the board of directors or another officer to the extent consistent with the bylaws.

V. RESIDENT AGENT
    A. A corporation must register an agent with the state who has an office within the state.

VI. FILING FEES
    A. Articles of Incorporation
       (not over $100,000 in capital stock) $20.00
    B. Change of Resident Agent & Acceptance $10.00
    C. Application for Name Reservation $7.00
    D. Amending Articles of Incorporation (minimum) $20.00
    E. Filing Annual Report $100.00
    F. Cost for Certified Copy of Any Document $6.00 + $1.00/page
    G. Recording Fee $20.00
    H. Expedited services $9.00 - $30.00

Note: The minimum filing fee to initially incorporate is $40.00, which includes the filing of the Articles of Incorporation and the Recording Fee.

MASSACHUSETTS

Chapter 156, Massachusetts General Laws

Secretary of State
Corporations Division
One Ashburton Place
17th Floor
Boston, MA 02108-1512
(617) 727-9640 or (617) 727-9440
Citizen Information Service
(800) 392-6090

Web site: http://www.state.ma.us/sec/cor/coridx.htm

I.   ARTICLES OF ORGANIZATION
    A.   Must provide state corporation office with the original Articles.

II. THE CORPORATE NAME
    A.   Name must indicate that the business is a corporation by using such words as "corporation," "incorporated," or abbreviation of the same.
    B.   Prior to incorporation, a corporate name may be reserved for a period of 30 days. Name availability may be checked by telephone but may be reserved only upon written request and payment of reservation fee.

III. DIRECTORS
    A.   Directors need not be residents of the state or shareholders of the corporation.
    B.   The articles or bylaws may prescribe additional requirements or qualifications.
    C.   A corporation must have three directors or more as initially stated in articles and thereafter as many directors as stated in bylaws. However, when there are less than three shareholders, there need be only a corresponding number of directors.
    D.   Director(s) are normally elected at the annual meeting of shareholders.
    E.   The president must also be a director unless otherwise provided in the bylaws.

IV. OFFICERS
    A.   A corporation must have a president, treasurer and clerk. Other officers may be elected or appointed in accordance with provisions set forth in the bylaws.
    B.   The same person may hold more than one office unless provided for otherwise in the bylaws.
    C.   An officer performs duties stated in the bylaws or by the board of directors or another officer to the extent consistent with the bylaws.
    D.   The clerk shall be responsible for preparing the records of any director or shareholder meeting.

V.   RESIDENT (REGISTERED) AGENT
    A.   A corporation must register an agent with the state who has an office within the state.

VI. FILING FEES
A. Articles of Organization	$200.00 minimum
B. Change of Registered Agent's Name/Address	no fee
C. Application for Name Reservation	$15.00
D. Amending Articles of Incorporation	$100.00 minimum
E. Filing Annual Report	$85.00 ($110.00 if not timely filed)
F. Cost for Certified Copy of Articles	$12.00
G. Cost for Certified Copy of Any Other Document	$7.00/first page + $2.00/additional page

MICHIGAN

Chapter 450, Michigan Compiled Laws

Michigan Department of Commerce
Corporation and Securities Bureau,
Corporation Division
6546 Mercantile Way
P.O. Box 30054
Lansing, MI 48909-7554
(517) 241-6420

Web site: http://www.cis.state.mi.us/corp/

I.   ARTICLES OF INCORPORATION
   A.   Must be printed or typewritten in English.
   B.   Must provide state corporation office with the original and one exact copy of the Articles.

II. THE CORPORATE NAME
   A.   Name must contain the word "corporation," "incorporated," "company," "limited," or abbreviation of the same.
   B.   Prior to incorporation, a corporate name may be reserved for a period of six full calendar months. Two two-month extensions are also available. Name must be reserved by written application.

III. DIRECTORS
   A.   Directors need not be residents of the state or shareholders of the corporation.
   B.   The articles or bylaws may prescribe additional requirements or qualifications.
   C.   A corporation must have one director or more as initially stated in articles and thereafter as many directors as stated in bylaws.
   D.   Director(s) are normally elected at the annual meeting of shareholders.

IV. OFFICERS
   A.   A corporation must have a president, secretary, treasurer, and may have a chairman of the board, and various vice presidents. Other officers may be elected or appointed in accordance with provisions set forth in the bylaws.
   B.   The same person may hold more than one office unless provided for otherwise in the bylaws.
   C.   An officer performs duties stated in the bylaws or by the board of directors or another officer to the extent consistent with the bylaws.

V.   RESIDENT AGENT
   A.   Corporation must register with the state a resident agent at an office within the state.

VI. FILING FEES
   A. Articles of Incorporation
        (60,000 shares or less of stock) $60.00
   B. Change of Registered Agent & Acceptance $5.00
   C. Application for Name Reservation $10.00
   D. Amending Articles of Incorporation $10.00
   E. Filing Annual Report $15.00

Minnesota

Chapter 302A Minnesota Statutes

Secretary of State
Division of Corporations
180 State Office Building
100 Constitution Ave.
St. Paul, MN 55155-1299
(651) 296-2803

Web site: http://www.sos.state.mn.us/bus.html

I. ARTICLES OF INCORPORATION
   A. Must provide state corporation office with the original Articles, typewritten or printed in black ink.

II. THE CORPORATE NAME
   A. Name must contain the word "corporation," "incorporated," "limited," or abbreviation of the same or the word "company" or its abbreviation, if it is not immediately preceded by "and" or "&".
   B. Prior to incorporation, a corporate name may be reserved for a period of 12 months.

III. DIRECTORS
   A. Directors need not be residents of the state or shareholders of the corporation.
   B. The articles or bylaws may prescribe additional requirements or qualifications.
   C. A corporation must have one director or more as initially stated in articles and thereafter as many directors as stated in bylaws.
   D. Director(s) are normally elected at the annual meeting of shareholders or in manner prescribed in bylaws.

IV. OFFICERS
   A. A corporation must have a chief executive officer and a chief financial officer, however designated. Other officers may be elected or appointed in accordance with provisions set forth in the bylaws.
   B. The same person may hold more than one office unless provided for otherwise in the bylaws.
   C. An officer performs duties stated in the bylaws or by the board of directors or another officer to the extent consistent with the bylaws.

V. REGISTERED AGENT
   A. A corporation must register an agent with the state who has an office within the state.

VI. FILING FEES
A. Articles of Incorporation	$135.00
B. Change of Registered Agent & Acceptance	no fee
C. Application for Name Reservation	$35.00
D. Amending Articles of Incorporation	$35.00
E. Filing Annual Report	no fee if timely filed
F. Cost for Certified Copy of Articles	$8.00
with Amendments	$11.00
G. Expedited Services	$20.00

MISSISSIPPI

Title 79, Mississippi Code

Secretary of State
Business Services Division
P.O. Box 136
Jackson, MS 39205-0136
Tel: (601) 359-1633
    (800) 256-3494
Fax:(601) 359-1499

Web site: http://www.sos.state.ms.us/

I.   ARTICLES OF INCORPORATION
     A.   Must be printed or typewritten in English.
     B.   Must provide state corporation office with the original and one exact copy of the Articles.

II. THE CORPORATE NAME
     A.   Name must contain the word "corporation," "incorporated," "company," "limited," or abbreviation of the same.
     B.   Prior to incorporation, a corporate name may be reserved for a period of 180 days.

III. DIRECTORS
     A.   Directors need not be residents of the state or shareholders of the corporation.
     B.   The articles or bylaws may prescribe additional requirements or qualifications.
     C.   The board of directors must consist of one or more individuals, initially stated in articles and with the number specified in or fixed in accordance with the articles or bylaws.
     D.   Director(s) are normally elected at the annual meeting of shareholders.

IV. OFFICERS
     A.   A corporation must have the officers described in its bylaws or appointed by the board of directors in accordance with provisions set forth in the bylaws.
     B.   The same person may hold more than one office unless provided for otherwise in the bylaws.
     C.   An officer performs duties stated in the bylaws or by the board of directors or another officer to the extent consistent with the bylaws.
     D.   One officer shall be responsible for preparing the records of any director or shareholder meeting.

V.   REGISTERED AGENT
     A.   A corporation must register an agent with the state who has an office within the state.

VI. FILING FEES
     A. Articles of Incorporation $50.00
     B. Change of Registered Agent's Name/Address $25.00
     C. Application for Name Reservation $25.00
     D. Amending Articles of Incorporation $50.00
     E. Filing Annual Report $25.00
     F. Cost for Certified Copy of Any Document $10.00/certificate + 1.00/page

Missouri

Chapter 351, Missouri Statutes

Secretary of State, Corporation Division
P.O. Box 778
Jefferson City, MO 65102
(573) 751-4153

Web site: http://mosl.sos.state.mo.us/bus-ser/soscor.html

I. ARTICLES OF INCORPORATION
   A. Must be printed or typewritten in English.
   B. Must provide state corporation office with duplicate originals of the Articles.

II. THE CORPORATE NAME
   A. Name must contain the word "corporation," "incorporated," "company," "limited," or abbreviation of the same.
   B. Prior to incorporation, a corporate name may be reserved for a period of 60 days. Name availability may be checked by telephone.

III. DIRECTORS
   A. Directors need not be residents of the state or shareholders of the corporation.
   B. The articles or bylaws may prescribe additional requirements or qualifications.
   C. A corporation must have three directors or more as initially stated in articles and thereafter as many directors as stated in bylaws. However, when there are less than three shareholders, there need be only a corresponding number of directors.
   D. Director(s) are normally elected at the annual meeting of shareholders.

IV. OFFICERS
   A. A corporation must have a president and secretary. Other officers may be elected or appointed in accordance with provisions set forth in the bylaws.
   B. The same person may hold more than one office unless provided for otherwise in the bylaws.
   C. An officer performs duties stated in the bylaws or by the board of directors to the extent consistent with the bylaws.

V. REGISTERED AGENT
   A. A corporation must register an agent with the state who has an office within the state.

VI. FILING FEES
   A. Articles of Incorporation
      (up to $30,000 shares of stock) $58.00
   B. Change of Registered Agent's Name/Address $10.00
   C. Application for Name Reservation $25.00
   D. Amending Articles of Incorporation $25.00
   E. Cost for Non-Certified Copy of Any Document $.50/page

MONTANA

Title 35, Montana Code

Secretary of State
P.O. Box 202801
Helena, MT 59620-2801
Tel: (406) 444-2034
Fax:(406) 444-3976

Web site: http://www.state.mt.us/sos/index.htm

I.   ARTICLES OF INCORPORATION
     A.   Must be printed or typewritten in English.
     B.   Must provide state corporation office with the original and one exact copy of the Articles.

II. THE CORPORATE NAME
     A.   Name must contain the word "corporation," "incorporated," "company," "limited," or abbreviation of the same.
     B.   Prior to incorporation, a corporate name may be reserved for a period of 120 days.

III. DIRECTORS
     A.   Directors need not be residents of the state or shareholders of the corporation.
     B.   The articles or bylaws may prescribe additional requirements or qualifications.
     C.   A corporation must have one director or more as initially stated in articles.
     D.   Director(s) are normally elected at the annual meeting of shareholders.

IV. OFFICERS
     A.   A corporation must have the officers described in its bylaws or as appointed by the board of directors in accordance with the bylaws.
     B.   The same person may hold more than one office.
     C.   An officer performs duties stated in the bylaws or by the board of directors or another officer to the extent consistent with the bylaws.

V.   REGISTERED AGENT
     A.   A corporation must register an agent with the state who has an office within the state.

VI. FILING FEES
     A. Articles of Incorporation $70.00*
     B. Change of Registered Agent's Name/Address $5.00
     C. Application for Name Reservation $10.00
     D. Amending Articles of Incorporation $15.00
     E. Filing Annual Report $10.00
     F. Cost for Certified Copy of Any Document $2.00 + .50 per page

*Note: At the time of incorporation, a domestic corporation must pay a license fee of a minimum of $70.00. This fee will give the corporation the authority to issue up to $50,000 worth of shares.

NEBRASKA

Chapter 21, Revised Nebraska Statutes

Secretary of State
Room 1305
P.O. Box 94608
Lincoln, NE 68509-4608
Tel: (402) 471-4079
Fax:(402) 471-3666

Web site: http://www.nol.org/home/SOS/htm/services.htm

I. ARTICLES OF INCORPORATION
    A. Must be printed or typewritten in English.
    B. Must provide state corporation office with the original and one exact copy of the Articles.

II. THE CORPORATE NAME
    A. Name must contain the word "corporation," "incorporated," "company," "limited," or abbreviation of the same.
    B. Prior to incorporation, a corporate name may be reserved for a period of 120 days.

III. DIRECTORS
    A. Directors need not be residents of the state or shareholders of the corporation.
    B. The articles or bylaws may prescribe additional requirements or qualifications.
    C. A corporation must have one director or more as initially stated in bylaws.
    D. Director(s) are normally elected at the annual meeting of shareholders.

IV. OFFICERS
    A. A corporation must have the offices as described in the bylaws or as appointed by the Board of Directors in accordance with the bylaws.
    B. The same person may hold more than one office.
    C. An officer performs duties stated in the bylaws or by the board of directors to the extent consistent with the bylaws.

V. REGISTERED AGENT
    A. A corporation must register an agent with the state who has an office within the state.

VI. FILING FEES

A. Articles of Incorporation (not over $10,000.00 of capital stock)	$60.00
B. Change of Registered Agent's Name/Address	$25.00
C. Application for Name Reservation	$25.00
D. Amending Articles of Incorporation	$25.00 + $5.00 per page
E. Cost for Certified Copy of Any Document	$10.00 + $1.00 per page

NEVADA

Chapter 78, Nevada Revised Statutes

Secretary of State
101 N. Carson Street, Suite 3
Carson City, NV 89710
Tel: (775) 684-5708

Web site: http://sos.state.nv.us

I. ARTICLES OF INCORPORATION
    A. Must provide state corporation office with the original and one exact copy of the Articles, typed or written in black ink.

II. THE CORPORATE NAME
    A. Any name which appears to be that of a natural person must contain the word "corporation," "incorporated," "company," "limited," or abbreviation of the same or any other word that identifies the name as not being that of a natural person.
    B. Prior to incorporation, a corporate name may be reserved for a period of 90 days.

III. DIRECTORS
    A. Directors need not be residents of the state or shareholders of the corporation.
    B. The articles or bylaws may prescribe additional requirements or qualifications.
    C. A corporation must have one director or more as initially stated in articles and thereafter as many directors as stated in bylaws.
    D. Director(s) are normally elected at the annual meeting of shareholders.

IV. OFFICERS
    A. A corporation must have a president, secretary, and treasurer. Other officers may be elected or appointed in accordance with provisions set forth in the bylaws.
    B. The same person may hold more than one office unless provided for otherwise in the bylaws.
    C. An officer performs duties stated in the bylaws or by the board of directors to the extent consistent with the bylaws.

V. REGISTERED AGENT
    A. A corporation must register an agent with the state who has an office within the state.

VI. FILING FEES
    A. Articles of Incorporation
        ($25,000 or less of capital stock) $125.00
    B. Change of Registered Agent's
        Name/Address $15.00
    C. Application for Name Reservation $20.00
    D. Amending Articles of Incorporation $75.00
    E. Filing Annual Report $85.00
    F. Cost for Certified Copy of Articles
        when a copy is provided $10.00
    G. Expedited Services $50.00

NEW HAMPSHIRE

Chapter 293-A, New Hampshire Revised Statutes

Secretary of State
Division of Corporations
State House, Room 204
107 N. Main St.
Concord, NH 03301
Tel: (603) 271-3244
Fax: (603) 271-3247

Web site: http://www.state.nh.us/sos/

I. ARTICLES OF INCORPORATION
    A. Must be printed or typewritten in English.
    B. Must provide state corporation office with the original and one exact copy of the Articles.

II. THE CORPORATE NAME
    A. Name must contain the word "corporation," "incorporated," "limited," or abbreviation of the same.
    B. Prior to incorporation, a corporate name may be reserved for a period of 120 days.

III. DIRECTORS
    A. Directors need not be residents of the state or shareholders of the corporation.
    B. The articles or bylaws may prescribe additional requirements or qualifications.
    C. A corporation must have one director or more as initially stated in bylaws.
    D. Director(s) are normally elected at the annual meeting of shareholders.

IV. OFFICERS
    A. A corporation must have the officers described in its bylaws or as appointed by the Board of Directors in accordance with the bylaws.
    B. The same person may hold more than one office.
    C. An officer performs duties stated in the bylaws or by the board of directors to the extent consistent with the bylaws.

V. REGISTERED AGENT
    A. A Corporation must register an agent with the state who has an office within the state.

VI. FILING FEES
    A. Articles of Incorporation
       (when authorized capital stock exceeds
       $10,000 but does not exceed $15,000) $160.00*
    B. Change of Registered Agent's Name/Address $15.00
    C. Application for Name Reservation $15.00
    D. Amending Articles of Incorporation $35.00
    E. Cost for Certified Copy of Any Document $5.00 + $1.00 per page
    F. Annual Report $100.00

*Minimum fee is $85.00 if authorized capital stock is 0-10 shares.

New Jersey

Title 14A, New Jersey Revised Statutes

Department of Treasury
Division of Corporate Filing
P.O. Box 308
Trenton, NJ 08625-0308
(609) 530-6400

Web site: http://www.state.nj.us/state/

I.   CERTIFICATE OF INCORPORATION
    A.   Must be printed or typewritten in English.
    B.   Must provide state corporation office with the original and one exact copy of the Certificate.

II. THE CORPORATE NAME
    A.   Name must contain the word "corporation," "incorporated," "company," abbreviation of the same, or "ltd."
    B.   Prior to incorporation, a corporate name may be reserved for a period of 120 days. Name must be reserved through written application.

III. DIRECTORS
    A.   Directors need not be residents of the state or shareholders of the corporation, but must be at least 18 years of age.
    B.   The certificate or bylaws may prescribe additional requirements or qualifications.
    C.   A corporation must have one director or more as initially stated in certificate and thereafter as many directors as stated in bylaws.
    D.   Director(s) are normally elected at the annual meeting of shareholders.

IV. OFFICERS
    A.   A corporation must have a president, secretary, and treasurer. Other officers may be elected.
    B.   The same person may hold more than one office unless provided for otherwise in the bylaws.
    C.   An officer performs duties stated in the bylaws or by the board of directors to the extent consistent with the bylaws.

V.   REGISTERED AGENT
    A.   A corporation must register an agent with the state who has an office within the state.

VI. FILING FEES

A. Articles of Incorporation	$100.00
B. Change of Registered Agent's Name/Address	$10.00
C. Application for Name Reservation	$50.00
D. Amending Certificate of Incorporation	$50.00
E. Filing Annual Report	$40.00
F. Expedited Services	$10.00
G. Same Day Service	$50.00

NEW MEXICO

Chapter 53, New Mexico Statutes

Public Regulation Commission
Corporation Department
P.O. Drawer 1269
Santa Fe, NM 87504-1269
(505) 827-4511

Web site: http://www.sos.state.nm.us/

I. ARTICLES OF INCORPORATION
    A. Must provide state corporation office with duplicate originals of the Articles.

II. THE CORPORATE NAME
    A. Name must contain the word "corporation," "incorporated," "company," "limited," or abbreviation of the same.
    B. Prior to incorporation, a corporate name may be reserved for a period of 120 days.

III. DIRECTORS
    A. Directors need not be residents of the state or shareholders of the corporation.
    B. The articles or bylaws may prescribe additional requirements or qualifications.
    C. A corporation must have one director or more as initially stated in articles and thereafter as many directors as stated in bylaws.
    D. Director(s) are normally elected at the annual meeting of shareholders.

IV. OFFICERS
    A. A corporation must have the officers described in its bylaws or appointed in accordance with provisions set forth in the bylaws.
    B. The same person may hold more than one office unless provided for otherwise in the bylaws.
    C. An officer performs duties stated in the bylaws or by the board of directors to the extent consistent with the bylaws.
    D. One officer shall be responsible for preparing the records of any director or shareholder meeting.

V. REGISTERED AGENT
    A. A corporation must register an agent with the state who has an office within the state.

VI. FILING FEES
    A. Articles of Incorporation
        (up to $500,000.00 capital stock) $100.00
    B. Change of Registered Agent's Name/Address $25.00
    C. Application for Name Reservation $25.00
    D. Amending Articles of Incorporation $100.00
    E. Filing Annual Report $25.00
    F. Cost for Certified Copy of Any Document $10.00 + $1.00/page

NEW YORK

Chapter 4, Consolidated Laws of New York

> Department of State
> Division of Corporations and State Records
> 41 State Street
> Albany, N.Y. 12231
> (518) 473-2492

> Web site: http://www.dos.state.ny.us/

I. CERTIFICATE OF INCORPORATION
    A. Must be printed or typewritten in English.
    B. Must provide state corporation office with the original certificate. State send certified copy to county where corporation is to be located.

II. THE CORPORATE NAME
    A. Name must contain the word "corporation," "incorporated," "limited," or abbreviation of the same. The name cannot include the following words and phrases: board of trade, chamber of commerce, community renewal, state police, state trooper, tenant relocation, urban development, urban relocation, acceptance, annuity, assurance, bank, benefit, bond, casualty, doctor, endowment, fidelity, finance, guaranty, indemnity, insurance, investment, lawyer, loan, mortgage, savings, surety, title, trust, or underwriter.
    B. Prior to incorporation, a corporate name may be reserved for a period of 60 days. Name must be reserved through written application and can be renewed upon written request.

III. DIRECTORS
    A. Directors need not be residents of the state or shareholders of the corporation, but must be at least 18 years of age.
    B. The articles or bylaws may prescribe additional requirements or qualifications.
    C. A corporation must have one director or more as initially stated in articles and thereafter as many directors as stated in bylaws.
    D. Director(s) are normally elected at the annual meeting of shareholders.

IV. OFFICERS
    A. A corporation may have such officers as may be elected or appointed in accordance with provisions set forth in the bylaws.
    B. The same person may hold more than one office.
    C. An officer performs duties stated in the bylaws or by the board of directors to the extent consistent with the bylaws.

V. REGISTERED AGENT
    A. The Secretary of State must be designated as agent for the corporation to accept service of process. The corporation may register an agent with the state who has an office within the state.

VI. FILING FEES
    A. Certificate of Incorporation $135.00*
    B. Certificate of Change of Registered Agent's Name/Address $30.00
    C. Application for Name Reservation $20.00
    D. Amending Certificate of Incorporation $60.00
    E. Cost for Certified Copy of Any Document $10.00

*This fee includes a minimum tax of $10.00 for issuance of up to 200 shares of no par value stock. The tax will be higher if more shares are issued.

NORTH CAROLINA

Chapter 55, General Statutes of North Carolina

Department of Secretary of State
Corporations Division
P.O. Box 22622
Raleigh, NC 27626-0622
Tel: (919) 807-2225
Fax: (919) 807-2039

Web site: http://www.state.nc.us/secstate/

I. ARTICLES OF INCORPORATION
    A. Must be printed or typewritten in English.
    B. Must provide state corporation office with the original and one exact copy of the Articles.

II. THE CORPORATE NAME
    A. Name must contain the word "corporation," "incorporated," "company," "limited," or abbreviation of the same.
    B. Prior to incorporation, a corporate name may be reserved for a period of 120 days.

III. DIRECTORS
    A. Directors need not be residents of the state or shareholders of the corporation.
    B. The articles or bylaws may prescribe additional requirements or qualifications.
    C. A corporation must have one director or more as initially stated in articles.
    D. Director(s) are normally elected at the annual meeting of shareholders.

IV. OFFICERS
    A. A corporation must have the officers as provided in accordance with provisions set forth in the bylaws.
    B. The same person may hold more than one office unless provided for otherwise in the bylaws. No one person may act in more than one capacity where an action by two or more officers is required.
    C. An officer performs duties stated in the bylaws or by the board of directors or another officer to the extent consistent with the bylaws.
    D. One officer shall be responsible for maintaining and authenticating the records of the corporations.

V. REGISTERED AGENT
    A. Corporation must register with the state agent at an office within the state.

VI. FILING FEES
    A. Articles of Incorporation $125.00
    B. Change of Registered Agent's Name/Address $5.00
    C. Application for Name Reservation $10.00
    D. Amending Articles of Incorporation $50.00
    E. Filing Annual Report $20.00
    F. Cost for Certified Copy of Any Document $5.00 + $1.00 per page

NORTH DAKOTA

Title 10, North Dakota Century Code

> Secretary of State
> Capitol Building
> 600 East Boulevard Avenue
> Bismarck, ND 58505-0500
> Tel: (701) 328-4284 or (800) 352-0867 ext. 4284
> Fax: (701) 328-2992
>
> Web site: http://www.state.nd.us/sec

I. ARTICLES OF INCORPORATION
    A. Must be in English.
    B. Must provide state corporation office with the original of the Articles.

II. THE CORPORATE NAME
    A. Name must contain the word "corporation," "incorporated," "company," "limited," or abbreviation of the same.
    B. Prior to incorporation, a corporate name may be reserved for a period of 12 months.

III. DIRECTORS
    A. Directors need not be residents of the state or shareholders of the corporation.
    B. The articles or bylaws may prescribe additional requirements or qualifications.
    C. A corporation must have one director or more as initially stated in articles and thereafter as many directors as stated in bylaws.
    D. Director(s) are normally elected at the annual meeting of shareholders unless there is a fixed term as prescribed in the bylaws.

IV. OFFICERS
    A. A corporation must have a president, one or more vice presidents, a secretary and a treasurer. Other officers may be elected or appointed in accordance with provisions set forth in the bylaws.
    B. The same person may hold more than one office unless provided for otherwise in the bylaws.
    C. An officer performs duties stated in the bylaws or by the board of directors to the extent consistent with the bylaws.
    D. One officer shall be responsible for preparing the records of any director or shareholder meeting.

V. REGISTERED AGENT
    A. A corporation must register an agent with the state who has an office within the state and provide the state with his social security number or federal ID number.

VI. FILING FEES
A. Articles of Incorporation	$30.00*
B. Designation of Registered Agent	$10.00
C. License Fee (first $50,000 of stock)	$50.00
D. Application for Name Reservation	$10.00
E. Amending Articles of Incorporation	$20.00
F. Filing Annual Report	$25.00
G. Cost for Certified Copy of Any Document	$15.00 + $1.00/4 pgs

* A minimum of $90.00 is required to incorporate. This includes the filing fee, license fee, and designation of registered agent.

Oʜɪᴏ

Title 17, Ohio Revised Statutes

Secretary of State
Business Services Division
180 E. Broad St., 16th Floor
Columbus, OH 43215
(614) 466-3910

Web site: http://www.state.oh.us/sos/

I. ARTICLES OF INCORPORATION
    A. Must provide state corporation office with the original and one exact copy of the Articles.

II. THE CORPORATE NAME
    A. Name must contain the word "corporation," "incorporated," "company," or abbreviation of the same.
    B. Prior to incorporation, a corporate name may be reserved for a period of 60 days. Name must be reserved through written application and payment of fee. Name availability may be checked over the telephone.

III. DIRECTORS
    A. Directors need not be residents of the state or shareholders of the corporation.
    B. The articles or bylaws may prescribe additional requirements or qualifications.
    C. A corporation must have three directors or more as initially stated in articles and thereafter as many directors as stated in bylaws. However, when there are less than three shareholders, there need be only a corresponding number of directors.
    D. Director(s) are normally elected at the annual meeting of shareholders.

IV. OFFICERS
    A. A corporation must have a president, secretary, and treasurer. Other officers may be elected by the board of directors.
    B. The same person may hold more than one office unless provided for otherwise in the bylaws.
    C. An officer performs duties as determined by the board of directors.

V. REGISTERED AGENT
    A. A corporation must register an agent with the state who has an office within the state.

VI. FILING FEES
    A. Articles of Incorporation (minimum fee) $85.00 Up to 850 shares
        10¢ per share 851-1000
        5¢ per share 1001-10,000
        2¢ per share 10,001-50,000
        1¢ per share 50,001-100,000
        1/2¢ per share 100,001-500,000
        1/4¢ per share over 500,000
    B. Change of Registered Agent's Name/Address $3.00
    C. Application for Name Reservation $5.00
    D. Amending Articles of Incorporation $35.00
    E. Annual Report $10.00
    F. Cost for Certified Copy of Any Document $5.00 + $1.00 per page

OKLAHOMA

Title 18, Oklahoma Statutes

Secretary of State-Corporation Division
2300 N. Lincoln, Room 101
Oklahoma City, OK 73105-4897
Tel: (405) 522-4560
Fax: (406) 521-3771

Web site: http://www.occ.state.ok.us/

I.   CERTIFICATE OF INCORPORATION
    A.   Must provide state corporation office with the original and one conformed copy of the Certificate.

II. THE CORPORATE NAME
    A.   Name must contain the word "association," "club," "corporation," "incorporated," "company," "fund," "foundation," "institute," "society," "union," "syndicate," "limited," or abbreviation of the same.
    B.   Prior to incorporation, a corporate name may be reserved for a period of 60 days. Name must be reserved through written application, but informal name check may be done over the telephone.

III. DIRECTORS
    A.   Directors need not be residents of the state or shareholders of the corporation.
    B.   The certificate or bylaws may prescribe additional requirements or qualifications.
    C.   A corporation must have one director or more as initially stated in the bylaws unless the number of directors is fixed by the certificate.
    D.   Director(s) are normally elected at the annual meeting of shareholders.

IV. OFFICERS
    A.   A corporation must have the offices as provided for by the bylaws.
    B.   The same person may hold more than one office unless provided for otherwise in the bylaws.
    C.   An officer performs duties stated in the bylaws or by the board of directors to the extent consistent with the bylaws.

V.   REGISTERED AGENT
    A.   A corporation must register an agent with the state who has an office within the state.

VI. FILING FEES
    A. Certificate of Incorporation (minimum) $50.00
    B. Change of Registered Agent's Name/Address $10.00
    C. Application for Name Reservation $10.00
    D. Amending Certificate of Incorporation $50.00
    E. Cost for Certified Copy of Any Document $5.00 + $1.00 per page

OREGON

Title 7, Oregon Revised Statutes

Corporation Division
State of Oregon
255 Capitol Street, N.E., Suite 151
Salem, OR 97310-1327
Tel: (503) 986-2200
Fax:(503) 378-4381

Web site: http://www.sos.state.or.us/

I. ARTICLES OF INCORPORATION
A. Must be printed or typewritten in English.
B. Must provide state corporation office with the original and one exact copy of the Articles. Articles need not be typed or printed, but must be legible.

II. THE CORPORATE NAME
A. Name must contain the word "corporation," "incorporation," "company," "limited," or abbreviation of the same.
B. Prior to incorporation, a corporate name may be reserved for a period of 120 days. Name must be reserved through written application.

III. DIRECTORS
A. Directors need not be residents of the state or shareholders of the corporation.
B. The articles or bylaws may prescribe additional requirements or qualifications.
C. A corporation must have one director or more as initially stated in articles and thereafter as many directors as stated in bylaws.
D. Director(s) are normally elected at the annual meeting of shareholders.

IV. OFFICERS
A. A corporation must have a president and secretary. Other officers may be elected or appointed in accordance with provisions set forth in the bylaws.
B. The same person may hold more than one office unless provided for otherwise in the bylaws.
C. An officer performs duties stated in the bylaws or by the board of directors or another officer to the extent consistent with the bylaws.
D. The secretary shall be responsible for preparing the records of any director or shareholder meeting.

V. REGISTERED AGENT
A. A corporation must register an agent with the state who has an office within the state.

VI. FILING FEES
A. Articles of Incorporation	$50.00
B. Change of Registered Agent's Name/Address	$10.00
C. Application for Name Reservation	$10.00
D. Amending Articles of Incorporation	$10.00
E. Filing Annual Report	$30.00
F. Cost for Certified Copy of Any Document	$15.00

PENNSYLVANIA

Title 19, Pennsylvania Statutes

Department of State
Corporation Bureau
308 North Office Building
Harrisburg, PA 17120
Tel: (717) 787-1057

Web site: http://www.dos.state.pa.us/corp.htm

I. ARTICLES OF INCORPORATION
A. Must be printed or typewritten in English.
B. Must provide state corporation office with the original copy of the Articles, along with docking statement.

II. THE CORPORATE NAME
A. Name must contain the word "corporation," "incorporated," "company," "limited," "association," "fund," "syndicate," or abbreviation of Co., Inc., or Ltd.
B. Prior to incorporation, a corporate name may be reserved for a period of 120 days. Name must be reserved through written application, accompanied by docketing statement.

III. DIRECTORS
A. Directors need not be a resident of the commonwealth or a shareholder of the corporation.
B. The articles or bylaws may prescribe additional requirements or qualifications.
C. A corporation must have one director or more as initially stated in articles and thereafter as many directors as stated in bylaws.
D. Director(s) are normally elected at the annual meeting of shareholders.

IV. OFFICERS
A. A corporation must have a president, secretary, and treasurer. Other officers may be elected or appointed in accordance with provisions set forth in the bylaws.
B. The same person may hold more than one office unless provided for otherwise in the bylaws.
C. An officer performs duties stated in the bylaws or by the board of directors to the extent consistent with the bylaws.

V. REGISTERED AGENT
A. Corporation need not have a registered agent, but must register with the state an office located in the state which can accept service of process.

VI. FILING FEES

A. Articles of Incorporation	$100.00
B. Change of Registered Agent's Name/Address	$52.00
C. Application for Name Reservation	$52.00
D. Amending Articles of Incorporation	$52.00
E. Cost for Certified Copy of Any Document	$40.00 fee + $2.00/page

RHODE ISLAND

Title 7, General Laws of Rhode Island

Secretary of State
Corporations Division
100 N. Main St., 1st Floor
Providence, RI 02903-1335
Tel: (401) 222-3040
Fax:(401) 277-1309

Web site: http://www.state.ri.us/corporations/

I.   ARTICLES OF INCORPORATION
  A.   Must provide state corporation office with the original and one exact copy of the Articles.

II. CORPORATE NAME
  A.   Name must contain the word "corporation," "incorporated," "company," "limited," or abbreviation of the same.
  B.   Prior to incorporation, a corporate name may be reserved for a period of 120 days. Name availability may be requested over the telephone but may only be reserved through written application.

III. DIRECTORS
  A.   Directors need not be residents of the state or shareholders of the corporation.
  B.   The articles or bylaws may prescribe additional requirements or qualifications.
  C.   A corporation must have three directors or more as initially stated in articles and thereafter as many directors as stated in bylaws. However, when there are less than three shareholders, there need be only a corresponding number of directors.
  D.   Director(s) are normally elected at the annual meeting of shareholders.

IV. OFFICERS
  A.   A corporation must have a president and secretary. Other officers may be elected or appointed in accordance with provisions set forth in the bylaws.
  B.   The same person may hold more than one office unless provided for otherwise in the bylaws.
  C.   An officer performs duties stated in the bylaws or by the board of directors to the extent consistent with the bylaws.

V.   REGISTERED AGENT
  A.   A corporation must register an agent with the state who has an office within the state.

VI. FILING FEES
  A. Articles of Incorporation (up to 8,000 shares) $150.00
  B. Change of Registered Agent's Name/Address $20.00
  C. Application for Name Reservation $50.00
  D. Amending Articles of Incorporation $50.00
  E. Filing Annual Report $50.00
  F. Cost for Certified Copy of Any Document $5.00 + .50 per page

SOUTH CAROLINA

Title 33, Code of Laws of South Carolina

Secretary of State
Division of Corporations
P.O. Box 11350
Columbia, SC 29211
Tel: (803) 734-2158
Fax: (803) 734-1614

Web site: http://www.leginfo.state.sc.us/secretary.html

I. ARTICLES OF INCORPORATION
    A. Must be printed or typewritten in English.
    B. Must provide state corporation office with the original copy of the Articles, in black ink. The Articles must be signed by an incorporator, accompanied by a certificate stating that the requirements have been complied with and that the corporation is organized for a lawful and proper purpose, signed by an attorney licensed in South Carolina.

II. THE CORPORATE NAME
    A. Name must contain the word "corporation," "incorporated," "company," "limited," or abbreviation of the same.
    B. Prior to incorporation, a corporate name may be reserved for a period of 120 days. Name must be reserved through written application.

III. DIRECTORS
    A. Directors need not be residents of the state or shareholders of the corporation.
    B. The articles or bylaws may prescribe additional requirements or qualifications.
    C. A corporation must have one director or more as initially stated in articles.
    D. Director(s) are normally elected at the annual meeting of shareholders.

IV. OFFICERS
    A. A corporation must have the offices as described in the bylaws or as appointed by the board of directors in accordance with the bylaws.
    B. The same person may hold more than one office unless provided for otherwise in the bylaws.
    C. An officer performs duties stated in the bylaws or by the board of directors or another officer to the extent consistent with the bylaws.
    D. One officer shall be responsible for preparing the records of any director or shareholder meeting.

V. REGISTERED AGENT
    A. A corporation must register an agent with the state who has an office within the state.

VI. FILING FEES
    A. Articles of Incorporation $135.00
    B. Change of Registered Agent's Name/Address $10.00
    C. Application for Name Reservation $10.00
    D. Amending Articles of Incorporation $110.00
    E. Filing Annual Report $25.00
    F. Cost for Certified Copy of Any Document $3.00 + $.50/page

SOUTH DAKOTA

Title 47, South Dakota Codified Laws

Secretary of State
State Capital
500 E. Capital Street
Pierre, SD 57501
Tel: (605) 773-4845
Fax: (605) 773-4550

Web site: http://www.state.sd.us/state/executive/sos/sos.htm

I.   ARTICLES OF INCORPORATION
    A.   Must provide state corporation office with the original and one exact copy of the Articles.
    B.   Corporation cannot start business until the value of at least $1,000 has been received for the issuance of shares.

II. THE CORPORATE NAME
    A.   Name must contain the word "corporation," "incorporated," "company," "limited," or abbreviation of the same.
    B.   Prior to incorporation, a corporate name may be reserved for a period of 120 days. Name must be reserved through written application.

III. DIRECTORS
    A.   Directors need not be residents of the state or shareholders of the corporation.
    B.   The articles or bylaws may prescribe additional requirements or qualifications.
    C.   A corporation must have one director or more as initially stated in articles and thereafter as many directors as stated in bylaws.
    D.   Director(s) are normally elected at the annual meeting of shareholders.

IV. OFFICERS
    A.   A corporation shall have the officers described in its bylaws or appointed by the board in accordance with provisions set forth in the bylaws.
    B.   The same person may hold more than one office unless provided for otherwise in the bylaws.
    C.   An officer performs duties stated in the bylaws or by the board of directors or another officer to the extent consistent with the bylaws.

V.   REGISTERED AGENT
    A.   A corporation must register an agent with the state who has an office within the state.

VI. FILING FEES
    A. Articles of Incorporation
        (25,000 shares of stock or less) $90.00
    B. Change of Registered Agent's Name/Address $10.00
    C. Application for Name Reservation $15.00
    D. Amending Articles of Incorporation $20.00
    E. Filing Annual Report $25.00
    F. Cost for Certified Copy of Any Document $5.00 + $1.00/page

TENNESSEE

Title 48, Tennessee Code

> Department of State
> Division of Business Services
> Suite 1800
> James K. Polk Building
> Nashville, TN 37243-0306
> Tel: (615) 741-0537
> Fax: (615) 741-7310
>
> Web site: http://www.state.tn.us/sos/index.htm

I.   CHARTER
   A. Must provide state corporation office with the original and one exact copy of the Charter.

II. THE CORPORATE NAME
   A. Name must contain the word "corporation," "incorporated," "company," or abbreviation of the same.
   B. Prior to incorporation, a corporate name may be reserved for a period of 4 months. Name must be reserved through written application.

III. DIRECTORS
   A. Directors need not be residents of the state or shareholders of the corporation.
   B. The charter or bylaws may prescribe additional requirements or qualifications.
   C. A corporation must have one director or more as initially stated in articles and thereafter as many directors as stated in bylaws.
   D. Director(s) are normally elected at the first annual meeting of shareholders and at each annual meeting thereafter.

IV. OFFICERS
   A. A corporation must have a president and secretary. Other officers may be elected or appointed in accordance with provisions set forth in the bylaws.
   B. The same person may hold more than one office unless provided for otherwise in the bylaws, except the offices of president and secretary.
   C. An officer performs duties stated in the bylaws or by the board of directors or another officer to the extent consistent with the bylaws.
   D. One officer shall be responsible for preparing the records of any director or shareholder meeting.

V.   REGISTERED AGENT
   A. A corporation must register an agent with the state who has an office within the state.

VI. FILING FEES
   A. Charter $100.00
   B. Application for Name Reservation $20.00
   C. Amending Charter $20.00
   D. Filing Annual Report $20.00
   E. Cost for Certified Copy of Any Document $20.00

Texas

Business Corporation Act of Texas, Texas Civil Statutes

> Secretary of State
> Corporation Division
> P.O. Box 13697
> Austin, TX 78711
> Tel: (512) 463-5555
>   (900) 263-0060 ($1.00 per minute - forms and filing information.)
> Fax: (512) 463-5709
>
> Web site: http://www.sos.state.tx.us/

I.   ARTICLES OF INCORPORATION
   A.   Must provide state corporation office with the original and one exact copy of the Articles.

II. THE CORPORATE NAME
   A.   Name must contain the word "corporation," "incorporated," "company," or abbreviation of the same.
   B.   Prior to incorporation, a corporate name may be reserved for a period of 120 days. Name availability may be checked over the telephone, but may only be reserved through written application.

III. DIRECTORS
   A.   Directors need not be residents of the state or shareholders of the corporation.
   B.   The articles or bylaws may prescribe additional requirements or qualifications.
   C.   A corporation must have one director or more as initially stated in articles and thereafter as many directors as stated in bylaws.
   D.   Director(s) are normally elected at the annual meeting of shareholders.

IV. OFFICERS
   A.   A corporation must have a president and secretary. Other officers may be elected or appointed in accordance with provisions set forth in the bylaws.
   B.   The same person may hold more than one office unless provided for otherwise in the bylaws.
   C.   An officer performs duties stated in the bylaws or by the board of directors or another officer to the extent consistent with the bylaws.
   D.   One officer shall be responsible for preparing the records of any director or shareholder meeting.

V.   REGISTERED AGENT
   A.   A corporation must register an agent with the state who has an office within the state.

VI. FILING FEES
   A. Articles of Incorporation $300.00
   B. Change of Address of Registered Agent $15.00
   C. Application for Name Reservation $40.00
   D. Amending Articles of Incorporation $150.00

UTAH

Title 16, Utah Code

> Department of Commerce
> Division of Corporations and Commercial Code
> P.O. Box 146705
> 160 E. 300 South
> Salt Lake City, UT 84114-6705
> Tel: (801) 530-4849
> Fax: (801) 530-6111
>
> Web site: http://www.state.ut.us/working/corpsearch.html - information on corporations

I. ARTICLES OF INCORPORATION
    A. Must provide state corporation office with the original and one exact copy of the Articles.

II. THE CORPORATE NAME
    A. Name must contain the word "corporation," "incorporated," "company," or abbreviation of the same.
    B. Prior to incorporation, a corporate name may be reserved for a period of 120 days.

III. DIRECTORS
    A. Directors need not be residents of the state or shareholders of the corporation.
    B. The articles or bylaws may prescribe additional requirements or qualifications.
    C. A corporation must have three directors or more as initially stated in articles and thereafter as many directors as stated in bylaws. However, when there are less than three shareholders, there need be only a corresponding number of directors.
    D. Director(s) are normally elected at the annual meeting of shareholders.

IV. OFFICERS
    A. A corporation must have at least one officer. Other officers may be elected or appointed in accordance with provisions set forth in the bylaws.
    B. The same person may hold more than one office in the corporation.
    C. An officer performs duties stated in the bylaws or by the board of directors to the extent consistent with the bylaws.
    D. One officer shall be responsible for preparing the records of any director or shareholder meeting.

V. REGISTERED AGENT
    A. A corporation must register an agent with the state who has an office within the state.

VI. FILING FEES
    A. Articles of Incorporation $50.00
    B. Application for Name Reservation $20.00
    C. Amending Articles of Incorporation $25.00
    E. Filing Annual Report $10.00
    F. Cost for Certified Copy of Any Document $10.00 + $.30/page
    G. Expedited Services $75.00

Vermont

Title 11A, Vermont Statutes

Secretary of State
Division of Corporations
81 River Street, Drawer 09
Montpelier, VT 05609-1104
Tel: (802) 828-2363
Fax: (802) 828-2853

Web site: http://www.sec.state.vt.us/

I. ARTICLES OF INCORPORATION
   A. Must be printed or typewritten in English.
   B. Must provide state corporation office with the original and one exact copy of the Articles.

II. THE CORPORATE NAME
   A. Name must contain the word "corporation," "incorporated," "company," "limited," or abbreviation of the same.
   B. Prior to incorporation, a corporate name may be reserved for a period of 120 days. Name must be reserved through written application.

III. DIRECTORS
   A. Directors need not be residents of the state or shareholders of the corporation.
   B. The articles or bylaws may prescribe additional requirements or qualifications.
   C. A corporation must have three directors or more as initially stated in articles and thereafter as many directors as stated in bylaws. However, when there are less than three shareholders, there need be only a corresponding number of directors.
   D. Director(s) are normally elected at the annual meeting of shareholders.

IV. OFFICERS
   A. A corporation must have a president and a secretary. Other officers may be elected or appointed in accordance with provisions set forth in the bylaws.
   B. The same person may hold more than one office except the offices of president and secretary.
   C. An officer performs duties as determined by the board of directors.
   D. One officer shall be responsible for preparing the records of any director or shareholder meeting.

V. REGISTERED AGENT
   A. A corporation must register an agent with the state who has an office within the state.

VI. FILING FEES
A. Articles of Incorporation	$75.00
B. Change of Registered Agent's Name/Address	$5.00
C. Application for Name Reservation	$20.00
D. Amending Articles of Incorporation	$25.00
E. Filing Annual Report	$25.00
F. Cost for Certified Copy of Any Document	$5.00 + $1.00 per page

VIRGINIA

Title 13.1, Code of Virginia

State Corporation Commission
P.O. Box 1197
Richmond, VA 23218
Tel: (804) 371-9733

Web site: http://www.state.va.us/scc/index.html

I.   ARTICLES OF INCORPORATION
    A.   Must be printed or typewritten in English.
    B.   Must provide state corporation office with the original and one exact copy of the Articles.

II. THE CORPORATE NAME
    A.   Name must contain the word "corporation," "incorporated," "company," "limited," or abbreviation of the same.
    B.   Prior to incorporation, a corporate name may be reserved for a period of 120 days. Name availability may be checked by telephone but may only be reserved by written application.

III. DIRECTORS
    A.   Directors need not be a resident of the commonwealth or a shareholder of the corporation.
    B.   The articles or bylaws may prescribe additional requirements or qualifications.
    C.   A corporation must have one director or more as initially stated in articles and thereafter as many directors as stated in bylaws.
    D.   Director(s) are normally elected at the annual meeting of shareholders.

IV. OFFICERS
    A.   A corporation must have the officers elected or appointed in accordance with the provisions set forth in the bylaws.
    B.   The same person may hold more than one office unless provided for otherwise in the bylaws.
    C.   An officer performs duties stated in the bylaws or by the board of directors or another officer to the extent consistent with the bylaws.

V.   REGISTERED AGENT
    A.   A corporation must register an agent with the state who has an office within the state.

VI. FILING FEES
    A. Articles of Incorporation
        (up to 25,000 shares of capital stock) $75.00
    B. Change of Registered Agent's Name/Address   No fee
    C. Application for Name Reservation $10.00
    D. Amending Articles of Incorporation $25.00
    E. Filing Annual Report   No charge
    F. Cost for Certified Copy of Any Document $1.00/page + $3.00/certificate

WASHINGTON

Title 23B, Revised Code of Washington

Secretary of State
Corporation Division
P.O. Box 40234
Olympia, WA 98504-0234
Tel: (360) 753-7115

Web site: http://www.secstate.wa.gov/

I.   ARTICLES OF INCORPORATION
   A.   Must be printed or typewritten in English.
   B.   Must provide state corporation office with the original and one exact copy of the Articles.

II. THE CORPORATE NAME
   A.   Name must contain the word "corporation," "incorporated," "company," "limited," or abbreviation of the same.
   B.   Prior to incorporation, a corporate name may be reserved for a period of 180 days.

III. DIRECTORS
   A.   Directors need not be residents of the state or shareholders of the corporation.
   B.   The articles or bylaws may prescribe additional requirements or qualifications.
   C.   A corporation must have one director or more with the number specified in or fixed in accordance with the articles or bylaws.
   D.   Director(s) are normally elected at the annual meeting of shareholders.

IV. OFFICERS
   A.   A corporation must have the officers elected or appointed in accordance with provisions set forth in the bylaws.
   B.   The same person may hold more than one office unless provided for otherwise in the bylaws.
   C.   An officer performs duties as stated in the bylaws or by the board of directors or another officer to the extent consistent with the bylaws.

V.   REGISTERED AGENT
   A.   A corporation must register an agent with the state who has an office within the state.

VI. FILING FEES
   A. Articles of Incorporation $175.00
   B. Expedited service fee for fast filing $20.00
   C. Application for Name Reservation $30.00
   D. Amending Articles of Incorporation $30.00
   E. Filing Annual Report $10.00
   F. Cost for Certified Copy of Any Document $10.00/certificate & .20/page
   G. Annual License Fee $59.00

WEST VIRGINIA

Chapter 31, West Virginia Code

Secretary of State
Corporations Division
Bldg. 1, Suite 157-K
1900 Kanawha Blvd. East
Charleston, WV 25305-0770
Tel: (304) 558-8000
Fax: (304) 559-0900

Web site: http://www.state.wv.us/sos/

I. ARTICLES OF INCORPORATION
    A. Must provide state corporation office with duplicate originals of the Articles.

II. THE CORPORATE NAME
    A. Name must contain the word "corporation," "incorporated," "company," "limited," or abbreviation of the same.
    B. Prior to incorporation, a corporate name may be reserved for a period of 120 days by written application. A corporate name may be reserved temporarily by telephone or in person for a period of 7 days.

III. DIRECTORS
    A. Directors need not be residents of the state or shareholders of the corporation.
    B. The articles or bylaws may prescribe additional requirements or qualifications.
    C. A corporation must have one director or more as initially stated in articles or bylaws.
    D. Director(s) are normally elected at the annual meeting of shareholders.

IV. OFFICERS
    A. A corporation must have a president, secretary and treasurer. Other officers may be elected or appointed in accordance with provisions set forth in the bylaws.
    B. The same person may hold more than one office, except those of president and secretary.
    C. An officer performs duties as stated in the bylaws or by the board of directors to the extent consistent with the bylaws.

V. REGISTERED AGENT
    A. Secretary of State accepts process for each corporation and he will mail process on to the corporation.

VI. FILING FEES
    A. Articles of Incorporation (up to 5,000 shares of stock) $63.00*
    B. Change of Name of Officer $15.00
    C. Application for Name Reservation $15.00
    D. Amending Articles of Incorporation
         (plus any increase in license tax) $25.00
    E. Filing Annual Report
         (plus license tax and attorney-in-fact fee) $10.00
    F. Cost for Certified Copy of Any Document $10.00

*Filing fees may vary depending on the month the articles are filed. The actual fee for filing may range from $63.00 to $92.00. Filing fees will also increase incrementally for corporations authorized to issue over 5,000 shares of stock.

WISCONSIN

Chapter 180, Wisconsin Statutes

Department of Financial Institutions
Division of Corporate and Consumer Services, Corporate Section
P.O. Box 7846
Madison, WI 53707
Tel: (608) 266-7577
Faxl: (608) 267-6813

Web site: http://www.state.wi.us/agencies/sos/

I. ARTICLES OF INCORPORATION
    A. Articles must be written in English.
    B. Must provide state corporation office with the original and one exact copy of the Articles.

II. THE CORPORATE NAME
    A. Name must contain the word "corporation," "incorporated," "company," "limited," or abbreviation of the same.
    B. Prior to incorporation, a corporate name may be reserved for a period of 120 days. Name may be reserved through written or telephone application.

III. DIRECTORS
    A. Directors need not be residents of the state or shareholders of the corporation.
    B. The articles or bylaws may prescribe additional requirements or qualifications.
    C. A corporation must have one director or more as initially stated in articles or bylaws.
    D. Director(s) are normally elected at the annual meeting of shareholders.

IV. OFFICERS
    A. A corporation must have the officers as elected or appointed in accordance with provisions set forth in the bylaws.
    B. The same person may hold more than one office unless provided for otherwise in the bylaws.
    C. An officer performs duties stated in the bylaws or by the board of directors or another officer to the extent consistent with the bylaws.

V. REGISTERED AGENT
    A. A corporation must register an agent with the state who has an office within the state.

VI. FILING FEES
    A. Articles of Incorporation
        (up to 9,000 shares for minimum fee) $90.00
    B. Change of Registered Agent's Name/Address $10.00
    C. Application for Name Reservation $15.00
    D. Telephone Application for Name Reservation $30.00
    E. Amending Articles of Incorporation
        (plus $.01 for each additional share created) $40.00
    F. Filing Annual Report $25.00
    G. Cost for Certified Copy of Any Document $5.00 + $.50/page

WYOMING

Title 17, Wyoming Statutes

Secretary of State
State Capitol Building
Cheyenne, WY 82002
Tel: (307) 777-7311 or (307) 777-7312
Fax:(307) 777-5339

Web site: http://soswy.state.wy.us/

I.   ARTICLES OF INCORPORATION
   A. Articles must be written in English.
   B. Must provide state corporation office with the original and one exact copy of the Articles.

II. THE CORPORATE NAME
   A. Name may not contain language stating or implying that the corporation is organized for an unlawful purpose.
   B. Prior to incorporation, a corporate name may be reserved for a period of 120 days. Name availability may be checked over the telephone, but must be reserved through written application.

III. DIRECTORS
   A. Directors need not be residents of the state or shareholders of the corporation.
   B. The articles or bylaws may prescribe additional requirements or qualifications.
   C. A corporation must have one director or more as initially specified in or fixed in accordance with the articles or bylaws.
   D. Director(s) are normally elected at the annual meeting of shareholders.

IV. OFFICERS
   A. A corporation has the officers as elected or appointed in accordance with provisions set forth in the bylaws.
   B. The same person may hold more than one office unless provided for otherwise in the bylaws.
   C. An officer performs duties stated in the bylaws or by the board of directors or another officer to the extent consistent with the bylaws.
   D. One officer shall be responsible for preparing the records of any director or shareholder meeting.

V.   REGISTERED AGENT
   A. A corporation must register an agent with the state who has an office within the state.
   B. Written consent of the registered agent must accompany filing.

VI. FILING FEES
   A. Articles of Incorporation $100.00
   B. Change of Registered Agent's Name/Address $50.00
   C. Application for Name Reservation $50.00
   D. Amending Articles of Incorporation $50.00
   E. Amending Articles of Incorporation to
       Change Corporate Name $50.00
   F. Filing Annual Report $25.00*
   G. Cost for Certified Copy of Any Document   .50**

*To renew registered agent plus minimum of $50.00 Annual Report License Tax.

**$.50/1st 10 pgs + $.15/pg thereafter + $3.00 certification.

STATE INCORPORATION FORMS

Forms 1 through 6 are the forms which must be filed with the secretary of state or corporation division to form a corporation.

Form 1 applies to the following states:

Alabama	Kansas	Ohio
Alaska†	Kentucky	Oregon
Arizona	Maryland	Pennsylvania
Arkansas	Michigan	Rhode Island
California	Minnesota	South Carolina
Colorado	Mississippi	Texas*
District of Columbia	Missouri	Utah*
Florida	Montana	Vermont
Georgia	Nebraska	Virginia‡
Idaho	Nevada	Washington
Illinois	New Hampshire	West Virginia
Indiana	New Mexico	Wisconsin
Iowa	North Carolina	Wyoming
	North Dakota	

*For Texas and Utah, document must state: "The corporation will not commence business until $1,000 has been received for issuance of stock." (can be paid in money, labor, or property)

†For Alaska, the document must state: "The name and address of each alien affiliate is: (if none, please indicate N/A)"_____

        name   complete resident or business address

‡For Virginia, the document must state that the registered agent is either (1.) a resident of Virginia and either a director of the corporation or a member of the Virginia Bar Association or (2.) a professional corporation or professional limited liability company rgistered under §54.1-3902.

Form 2 applies to the following state:

     Louisiana

Form 3 applies to the following states:

     Delaware

     Connecticut

     New Jersey

     New York

     Oklahoma

Form 4 applies to the following states:

     Maine

     Massachusetts

Form 5 applies to the following state:

     South Dakota

Form 6 applies to the following states:

     Hawaii

     Tennessee

STATE OF
_____

ARTICLES OF INCORPORATION
OF
_____,

A BUSINESS/STOCK CORPORATION

The name of the corporation is_____.

The business and mailing address of the corporation is_____
_____.
(street address, city, county, state, zip)

The duration of the corporation is perpetual.

The corporation has been organized to transact any and all lawful business for which corporations may be incorporated in this state.

The aggregate number of shares which the corporation shall have the authority to issue is_____ and the par value of each shall be _____. (typically "no par value")

The number of directors constituting the initial board of directors of the corporation is_____, and their names and addresses are:

The location and street address of the initial registered office is _____
_____ (must be located within the state) (list county also)
and the name of its initial registered agent at such address is _____

The name and address of each incorporator:

In witness thereof, the undersigned incorporator(s) have executed these articles of incorporation this _____day of _____, _____.

_____   _____
Witness   Incorporator

_____   _____
Witness   Incorporator

State of _____
County of_____

On _____, the above person(s) appeared before me, a notary public and are personally known or proved to me to be the person(s) whose name(s) is/are subscribed to the above instrument who acknowledged that he/she executed the instrument.

_____
Notary

(Notary stamp or seal)

115

This document prepared by:

_____

Consent of Appointment by the Registered Agent

I, _____, hereby give my consent to serve as the registered agent for

      (name of registered agent)

_____. Having been named as registered agent and to accept

      (corporate name)

service of process for the above stated corporation at the place designated in this certificate, I hereby accept the appointment as registered agent and agree to act in this capacity. I further agree to comply with the provisions of all statutes relating to the proper and complete performance of my duties, and am familiar with and accept the obligations of my position as registered agent.

Dated _____, _____.

                                               _____

                                               (signature of registered agent)

Articles prepared by:

STATE OF
_____

ARTICLES OF INCORPORATION
OF

_____ ,

A BUSINESS/STOCK CORPORATION

The name of the corporation is _____.

The business and mailing address of the corporation is _____
_____
(street address, city, county, state, zip)

The duration of the corporation is perpetual.

The corporation has been organized to transact any and all lawful business for which corporations may be incorporated in this state.

The aggregate number of shares which the corporation shall have the authority to issue is_____ and the par value of each shall be _____ (typically "no par value")

The location and street address of the initial registered office is _____
_____(must be located within the state) (list county also)
and the name of its initial registered agent at such address is_____.

The corporation's federal tax identification number is

The name and address of each incorporator:

In witness thereof, the undersigned incorporator(s) have executed these articles of incorporation this ____ day of _____, _____.

_____   _____
Witness   Incorporator
_____   _____
Witness   Incorporator
_____   _____
Witness   Incorporator

State of _____
County of _____

On_____ , the above person(s) appeared before me, a notary public, and are personally known or proved to me to be the person(s) whose name(s) is/are subscribed to the above instrument who acknowledged that he/she executed the instrument.

_____
Notary

(Notary stamp or seal)

This document prepared by:

STATE OF
_____

CERTIFICATE OF INCORPORATION
OF
_____ ,

A BUSINESS/STOCK CORPORATION

The name of the corporation is _____ .

The business and mailing address of the corporation is _____
_____
(street address, city, county, state, zip)

The duration of the corporation is perpetual.

The corporation has been organized to transact any and all lawful business for which corporations may be incorporated in this state.

The aggregate number of shares which the corporation shall have the authority to issue is_____ and the par value of each shall be _____ (typically "no par value")

The amount of the total authorized capitalized stock of this corporation is_____ Dollars ($_____) divided into _____ shares, of _____ Dollars ($_____).

The number of directors constituting the initial board of directors of the corporation is _____ , and their names and addresses are:

The location and street address of the initial registered office is _____
_____ (must be located within the state) (list county also)

and the name of its initial registered agent at such address is_____ .

The name and address of each incorporator:

In witness thereof, the undersigned incorporator(s) have executed this certificate of incorporation this _____ day of _____ , _____ .

_____
Incorporator

_____
Incorporator

State of _____

County of _____

On_____ , the above person(s) appeared before me, a notary public and are personally known or proved to me to be the person(s) whose name(s) is/are subscribed to the above instrument who acknowledged that he/she executed the instrument.

_____
Notary

(Notary stamp or seal)

This document prepared by:

STATE OF
_____

ARTICLES OF INCORPORATION
OF
_____ ,

A BUSINESS/STOCK CORPORATION

The name of the corporation is _____ .

The business and mailing address of the corporation is _____
_____
(street address, city, county, state, zip)
The duration of the corporation is perpetual.

The corporation has been organized to transact any and all lawful business for which corporations may be incorporated in this state.

The aggregate number of shares which the corporation shall have the authority to issue is_____ and the par value of each shall be _____ (typically "no par value")

The number of directors constituting the initial board of directors of the corporation is ____ , and their names and addresses are:

The location and street address of the initial registered office is _____
_____ (must be located within the state) (list county also)
and the name of its initial registered agent at such address is_____ .

The fiscal year shall be_____

The name and address of each officer:
Title   Name   Address
PRESIDENT
TREASURER
CLERK

The name and address of each incorporator:

In witness thereof, the undersigned incorporator(s) have executed these articles of incorporation this _____
day of _____, _____.

_____
Incorporator

_____
Incorporator

State of _____
County of _____

On_____ , the above person(s) appeared before me, a notary public and are personally known or proved to me to be the person(s) whose name(s) is/are subscribed to the above instrument who acknowledged that he/she executed the instrument.

_____
Notary

(Notary stamp or seal)
This document prepared by:

STATE OF

_____

ARTICLES OF INCORPORATION
OF

_____ ,

A BUSINESS/STOCK CORPORATION

The name of the corporation is _____ .

The business and mailing address of the corporation is _____

_____ (street address, city, county, state, zip)

The corporation has been organized to transact any and all lawful business for which corporations may be incorporated in this state.

The names of the initial subscribers for shares, the number of shares subscribed for, the subscription price and the amount of capital paid are as follows:

Name of initial subscribers:
1.
2.
3.

Number of shares subscribed for by each corresponding subscriber:
1.
2.
3.

Subscription price for the shares subscribed for by each subscriber:
1.
2.
3.

Amount of capital paid in cash by each subscriber:
1.
2.
3.

The name and address of each incorporator:

In witness thereof, the undersigned incorporator(s) have executed these articles of incorporation this _____ day of _____ , _____ .

_____
Incorporator

_____
Incorporator

State of _____

County of _____

On_____ , the above person(s) appeared before me, a notary public and are personally known or proved to me to be the person(s) whose name(s) is/are subscribed to the above instrument who acknowledged that he/she executed the instrument.

_____
Notary

(Notary stamp or seal)
This document prepared by:

STATE OF

_____

CHARTER
OF

_____ ,

A BUSINESS/STOCK CORPORATION

The name of the corporation is _____.

The business and mailing address of the corporation is _____
_____ (street address, city, county, state, zip)

The duration of the corporation is perpetual.

The corporation has been organized to transact any and all lawful business for which corporations may be incorporated in this state.

The aggregate number of shares which the corporation shall have the authority to issue is_____ and the par value of each shall be _____ (typically "no par value")

The corporation will not commence business until consideration of the value of at least One Thousand Dollars ($1,000.00) has been received for the issuance of shares.

The number of directors constituting the initial board of directors of the corporation is _____, and their names and addresses are:

The location and street address of the initial registered office is _____
_____ (must be located within the state) (list county also)
and the name of its initial registered agent at such address is_____.

The corporation's federal tax identification number is _____

The fiscal year shall be _____

The name and address of each officer:
<u>Title</u>   <u>Name</u>   <u>Address</u>

The name and address of each incorporator:

In witness thereof, the undersigned incorporator(s) have executed this charter this _____ day of
_____, _____.

_____
Incorporator

_____
Incorporator

State of _____

County of _____

On_____ , the above person(s) appeared before me, a notary public and are personally known or proved to me to be the person(s) whose name(s) is/are subscribed to the above instrument who acknowledged that he/she executed the instrument.

_____
Notary

(Notary stamp or seal)

_____

Consent of Appointment by the Registered Agent

I, _____ , hereby give my consent to serve as the registered agent for
(name of registered agent)

_____.
(corporate name)

Dated_____, _____.

_____
(signature of registered agent)

Articles prepared by:

APPENDIX C
CORPORATE FORMS

_____
(date)

_____
_____
_____
_____

Dear Sir or Madam:

Enclosed please find the necessary documents for the corporate registration of_____, along with a check in the amount of $_____ for the filing fee and any other required costs.

Also enclosed is a photocopy of the these corporate documents. Please return this to me with the filing date stamped on it.

Thank you,

_____

| Form **SS-4** (Rev. February 1998) Department of the Treasury Internal Revenue Service | **Application for Employer Identification Number** (For use by employers, corporations, partnerships, trusts, estates, churches, government agencies, certain individuals, and others. See instructions.) ► **Keep a copy for your records.** | EIN OMB No. 1545-0003 |

Please type or print clearly.

1 Name of applicant (legal name) (see instructions)

2 Trade name of business (if different from name on line 1)

3 Executor, trustee, "care of" name

4a Mailing address (street address) (room, apt., or suite no.)

5a Business address (if different from address on lines 4a and 4b)

4b City, state, and ZIP code

5b City, state, and ZIP code

6 County and state where principal business is located

7 Name of principal officer, general partner, grantor, owner, or trustor—SSN or ITIN may be required (see instructions) ►

8a Type of entity (Check only one box.) (see instructions)

Caution: *If applicant is a limited liability company, see the instructions for line 8a.*

- ☐ Sole proprietor (SSN) _____
- ☐ Partnership
- ☐ REMIC
- ☐ State/local government
- ☐ Church or church-controlled organization
- ☐ Other nonprofit organization (specify) ► _____
- ☐ Other (specify) ►

- ☐ Personal service corp.
- ☐ National Guard
- ☐ Farmers' cooperative

- ☐ Estate (SSN of decedent) _____
- ☐ Plan administrator (SSN) _____
- ☐ Other corporation (specify) ► _____
- ☐ Trust
- ☐ Federal government/military

(enter GEN if applicable) _____

8b If a corporation, name the state or foreign country (if applicable) where incorporated

| State | Foreign country |

9 Reason for applying (Check only one box.) (see instructions)
- ☐ Started new business (specify type) ► _____
- ☐ Hired employees (Check the box and see line 12.)
- ☐ Created a pension plan (specify type) ►
- ☐ Banking purpose (specify purpose) ► _____
- ☐ Changed type of organization (specify new type) ► _____
- ☐ Purchased going business
- ☐ Created a trust (specify type) ► _____
- ☐ Other (specify) ►

10 Date business started or acquired (month, day, year) (see instructions)

11 Closing month of accounting year (see instructions)

12 First date wages or annuities were paid or will be paid (month, day, year). **Note:** *If applicant is a withholding agent, enter date income will first be paid to nonresident alien. (month, day, year)* . . . . ►

13 Highest number of employees expected in the next 12 months. **Note:** *If the applicant does not expect to have any employees during the period, enter -0-. (see instructions)* . . . . ►

Nonagricultural	Agricultural	Household

14 Principal activity (see instructions) ►

15 Is the principal business activity manufacturing? . . . . ☐ Yes ☐ No
If "Yes," principal product and raw material used ►

16 To whom are most of the products or services sold? Please check one box.
☐ Business (wholesale)
☐ Public (retail) ☐ Other (specify) ► ☐ N/A

17a Has the applicant ever applied for an employer identification number for this or any other business? . . . . ☐ Yes ☐ No
Note: *If "Yes," please complete lines 17b and 17c.*

17b If you checked "Yes" on line 17a, give applicant's legal name and trade name shown on prior application, if different from line 1 or 2 above.
Legal name ► Trade name ►

17c Approximate date when and city and state where the application was filed. Enter previous employer identification number if known.

| Approximate date when filed (mo., day, year) | City and state where filed | Previous EIN |

Under penalties of perjury, I declare that I have examined this application, and to the best of my knowledge and belief, it is true, correct, and complete.

| Business telephone number (include area code) |
| Fax telephone number (include area code) |

Name and title (Please type or print clearly.) ►

Signature ► Date ►

Note: *Do not write below this line. For official use only.*

Please leave blank ►	Geo.	Ind.	Class	Size	Reason for applying

For Paperwork Reduction Act Notice, see page 4.   Cat. No. 16055N   Form **SS-4** (Rev. 2-98)

General Instructions

Section references are to the Internal Revenue Code unless otherwise noted.

Purpose of Form

Use Form SS-4 to apply for an employer identification number (EIN). An EIN is a nine-digit number (for example, 12-3456789) assigned to sole proprietors, corporations, partnerships, estates, trusts, and other entities for tax filing and reporting purposes. The information you provide on this form will establish your business tax account.

Caution: *An EIN is for use in connection with your business activities only. Do NOT use your EIN in place of your social security number (SSN).*

Who Must File

You must file this form if you have not been assigned an EIN before and:

● You pay wages to one or more employees including household employees.

● You are required to have an EIN to use on any return, statement, or other document, even if you are not an employer.

● You are a withholding agent required to withhold taxes on income, other than wages, paid to a nonresident alien (individual, corporation, partnership, etc.). A withholding agent may be an agent, broker, fiduciary, manager, tenant, or spouse, and is required to file **Form 1042,** Annual Withholding Tax Return for U.S. Source Income of Foreign Persons.

● You file **Schedule C,** Profit or Loss From Business, **Schedule C-EZ,** Net Profit From Business, or **Schedule F,** Profit or Loss From Farming, of **Form 1040,** U.S. Individual Income Tax Return, **and** have a Keogh plan or are required to file excise, employment, or alcohol, tobacco, or firearms returns.

The following must use EINs even if they do not have any employees:

● State and local agencies who serve as tax reporting agents for public assistance recipients, under Rev. Proc. 80-4, 1980-1 C.B. 581, should obtain a separate EIN for this reporting. See **Household employer** on page 3.

● Trusts, except the following:

   1. Certain grantor-owned trusts. (See the **Instructions for Form 1041.**)

   2. Individual Retirement Arrangement (IRA) trusts, unless the trust has to file **Form 990-T,** Exempt Organization Business Income Tax Return. (See the **Instructions for Form 990-T.**)

● Estates

● Partnerships

● REMICs (real estate mortgage investment conduits) (See the **Instructions for Form 1066,** U.S. Real Estate Mortgage Investment Conduit Income Tax Return.)

● Corporations

● Nonprofit organizations (churches, clubs, etc.)

● Farmers' cooperatives

● Plan administrators (A plan administrator is the person or group of persons specified as the administrator by the instrument under which the plan is operated.)

When To Apply for a New EIN

New Business. If you become the new owner of an existing business, **do not** use the EIN of the former owner. IF YOU ALREADY HAVE AN EIN, USE THAT NUMBER. If you do not have an EIN, apply for one on this form. If you become the "owner" of a corporation by acquiring its stock, use the corporation's EIN.

Changes in Organization or Ownership. If you already have an EIN, you may need to get a new one if either the organization or ownership of your business changes. If you incorporate a sole proprietorship or form a partnership, you must get a new EIN. However, **do not** apply for a new EIN if:

● You change only the name of your business,

● You elected on **Form 8832,** Entity Classification Election, to change the way the entity is taxed, or

● A partnership terminates because at least 50% of the total interests in partnership capital and profits were sold or exchanged within a 12-month period. (See Regulations section 301.6109-1(d)(2)(iii).) The EIN for the terminated partnership should continue to be used. This rule applies to terminations occurring after May 8, 1997. If the termination took place after May 8, 1996, and before May 9, 1997, a new EIN must be obtained for the new partnership unless the partnership and its partners are consistent in using the old EIN.

Note: *If you are electing to be an "S corporation," be sure you file **Form 2553,** Election by a Small Business Corporation.*

File Only One Form SS-4. File only one Form SS-4, regardless of the number of businesses operated or trade names under which a business operates. However, each corporation in an affiliated group must file a separate application.

EIN Applied for, But Not Received. If you do not have an EIN by the time a return is due, write "Applied for" and the date you applied in the space shown for the number. **Do not** show your social security number (SSN) as an EIN on returns.

If you do not have an EIN by the time a tax deposit is due, send your payment to the Internal Revenue Service Center for your filing area. (See **Where To Apply** below.) Make your check or money order payable to Internal Revenue Service and show your name (as shown on Form SS-4), address, type of tax, period covered, and date you applied for an EIN. Send an explanation with the deposit.

For more information about EINs, see **Pub. 583,** Starting a Business and Keeping Records, and **Pub. 1635,** Understanding your EIN.

How To Apply

You can apply for an EIN either by mail or by telephone. You can get an EIN immediately by calling the Tele-TIN number for the service center for your state, or you can send the completed Form SS-4 directly to the service center to receive your EIN by mail.

Application by Tele-TIN. Under the Tele-TIN program, you can receive your EIN by telephone and use it immediately to file a return or make a payment. To receive an EIN by telephone, complete Form SS-4, then call the Tele-TIN number listed for your state under **Where To Apply.** The person making the call must be authorized to sign the form. (See **Signature** on page 4.)

An IRS representative will use the information from the Form SS-4 to establish your account and assign you an EIN. Write the number you are given on the upper right corner of the form and sign and date it.

*Mail or fax (facsimile) the signed SS-4 **within 24 hours** to the Tele-TIN Unit at the service center address for your state. The IRS representative will give you the fax number. The fax numbers are also listed in Pub. 1635.*

Taxpayer representatives can receive their client's EIN by telephone if they first send a fax of a completed **Form 2848,** Power of Attorney and Declaration of Representative, or **Form 8821,** Tax Information Authorization, to the Tele-TIN unit. The Form 2848 or Form 8821 will be used solely to release the EIN to the representative authorized on the form.

Application by Mail. Complete Form SS-4 at least 4 to 5 weeks before you will need an EIN. Sign and date the application and mail it to the service center address for your state. You will receive your EIN in the mail in approximately 4 weeks.

Where To Apply

The Tele-TIN numbers listed below will involve a long-distance charge to callers outside of the local calling area and can be used only to apply for an EIN. THE NUMBERS MAY CHANGE WITHOUT NOTICE. Call 1-800-829-1040 to verify a number or to ask about the status of an application by mail.

If your principal business, office or agency, or legal residence in the case of an individual, is located in: ▼	Call the Tele-TIN number shown or file with the Internal Revenue Service Center at: ▼
Florida, Georgia, South Carolina	Attn: Entity Control Atlanta, GA 39901 770-455-2360
New Jersey, New York City and counties of Nassau, Rockland, Suffolk, and Westchester	Attn: Entity Control Holtsville, NY 00501 516-447-4955
New York (all other counties), Connecticut, Maine, Massachusetts, New Hampshire, Rhode Island, Vermont	Attn: Entity Control Andover, MA 05501 978-474-9717
Illinois, Iowa, Minnesota, Missouri, Wisconsin	Attn: Entity Control Stop 6800 2306 E. Bannister Rd. Kansas City, MO 64999 816-926-5999
Delaware, District of Columbia, Maryland, Pennsylvania, Virginia	Attn: Entity Control Philadelphia, PA 19255 215-516-6999
Indiana, Kentucky, Michigan, Ohio, West Virginia	Attn: Entity Control Cincinnati, OH 45999 606-292-5467

Kansas, New Mexico, Oklahoma, Texas	Attn: Entity Control Austin, TX 73301 512-460-7843
Alaska, Arizona, California (counties of Alpine, Amador, Butte, Calaveras, Colusa, Contra Costa, Del Norte, El Dorado, Glenn, Humboldt, Lake, Lassen, Marin, Mendocino, Modoc, Napa, Nevada, Placer, Plumas, Sacramento, San Joaquin, Shasta, Sierra, Siskiyou, Solano, Sonoma, Sutter, Tehama, Trinity, Yolo, and Yuba), Colorado, Idaho, Montana, Nebraska, Nevada, North Dakota, Oregon, South Dakota, Utah, Washington, Wyoming	Attn: Entity Control Mail Stop 6271 P.O. Box 9941 Ogden, UT 84201 801-620-7645
California (all other counties), Hawaii	Attn: Entity Control Fresno, CA 93888 209-452-4010
Alabama, Arkansas, Louisiana, Mississippi, North Carolina, Tennessee	Attn: Entity Control Memphis, TN 37501 901-546-3920
If you have no legal residence, principal place of business, or principal office or agency in any state	Attn: Entity Control Philadelphia, PA 19255 215-516-6999

Specific Instructions

The instructions that follow are for those items that are not self-explanatory. Enter N/A (nonapplicable) on the lines that do not apply.

Line 1. Enter the legal name of the entity applying for the EIN exactly as it appears on the social security card, charter, or other applicable legal document.

Individuals. Enter your first name, middle initial, and last name. If you are a sole proprietor, enter your individual name, not your business name. Enter your business name on line 2. Do not use abbreviations or nicknames on line 1.

Trusts. Enter the name of the trust.

Estate of a decedent. Enter the name of the estate.

Partnerships. Enter the legal name of the partnership as it appears in the partnership agreement. **Do not** list the names of the partners on line 1. See the specific instructions for line 7.

Corporations. Enter the corporate name as it appears in the corporation charter or other legal document creating it.

Plan administrators. Enter the name of the plan administrator. A plan administrator who already has an EIN should use that number.

Line 2. Enter the trade name of the business if different from the legal name. The trade name is the "doing business as" name.

Note: *Use the full legal name on line 1 on all tax returns filed for the entity. However, if you enter a trade name on line 2 and choose to use the trade name instead of the legal name, enter the trade name on all returns you file. To prevent processing delays and errors, always use either the legal name only or the trade name only on all tax returns.*

Line 3. Trusts enter the name of the trustee. Estates enter the name of the executor, administrator, or other fiduciary. If the entity applying has a designated person to receive tax information, enter that person's name as the "care of" person. Print or type the first name, middle initial, and last name.

Line 7. Enter the first name, middle initial, last name, and SSN of a principal officer if the business is a corporation; of a general partner if a partnership; of the owner of a single member entity that is disregarded as an entity separate from its owner; or of a grantor, owner, or trustor if a trust. If the person in question is an alien individual with a previously assigned individual taxpayer identification number (ITIN), enter the ITIN in the space provided, instead of an SSN. You are not required to enter an SSN or ITIN if the reason you are applying for an EIN is to make an entity classification election (see Regulations section 301.7701-1 through 301.7701-3), and you are a nonresident alien with no effectively connected income from sources within the United States.

Line 8a. Check the box that best describes the type of entity applying for the EIN. If you are an alien individual with an ITIN previously assigned to you, enter the ITIN in place of a requested SSN.

Caution: *This is not an election for a tax classification of an entity. See "Limited liability company" below.*

If not specifically mentioned, check the "Other" box, enter the type of entity and the type of return that will be filed (for example, common trust fund, Form 1065). Do not enter N/A. If you are an alien individual applying for an EIN, see the **Line 7** instructions above.

Sole proprietor. Check this box if you file Schedule C, C-EZ, or F (Form 1040) and have a Keogh plan, or are required to file excise, employment, or alcohol, tobacco, or firearms returns, or are a payer of gambling winnings. Enter your SSN (or ITIN) in the space provided. If you are a nonresident alien with no effectively connected income from sources within the United States, you do not need to enter an SSN or ITIN.

REMIC. Check this box if the entity has elected to be treated as a real estate mortgage investment conduit (REMIC). See the **Instructions for Form 1066** for more information.

Other nonprofit organization. Check this box if the nonprofit organization is other than a church or church-controlled organization and specify the type of nonprofit organization (for example, an educational organization).

If the organization also seeks tax-exempt status, you must file either **Package 1023**, Application for Recognition of Exemption, or **Package 1024**, Application for Recognition of Exemption Under Section 501(a). Get **Pub. 557**, Tax Exempt Status for Your Organization, for more information.

Group exemption number (GEN). If the organization is covered by a group exemption letter, enter the four-digit GEN. (Do not confuse the GEN with the nine-digit EIN.) If you do not know the GEN, contact the parent organization. Get Pub. 557 for more information about group exemption numbers.

Withholding agent. If you are a withholding agent required to file Form 1042, check the "Other" box and enter "Withholding agent."

Personal service corporation. Check this box if the entity is a personal service corporation. An entity is a personal service corporation for a tax year only if:

● The principal activity of the entity during the testing period (prior tax year) for the tax year is the performance of personal services substantially by employee-owners, and

● The employee-owners own at least 10% of the fair market value of the outstanding stock in the entity on the last day of the testing period.

Personal services include performance of services in such fields as health, law, accounting, or consulting. For more information about personal service corporations, see the **Instructions for Form 1120**, U.S. Corporation Income Tax Return, and **Pub. 542**, Corporations.

Limited liability company (LLC). See the definition of limited liability company in the **Instructions for Form 1065**. An LLC with two or more members can be a partnership or an association taxable as a corporation. An LLC with a single owner can be an association taxable as a corporation or an entity disregarded as an entity separate from its owner. See Form 8832 for more details.

● If the entity is classified as a partnership for Federal income tax purposes, check the "partnership" box.

● If the entity is classified as a corporation for Federal income tax purposes, mark the "Other corporation" box and write "limited liability co." in the space provided.

● If the entity is disregarded as an entity separate from its owner, check the "Other" box and write in "disregarded entity" in the space provided.

Plan administrator. If the plan administrator is an individual, enter the plan administrator's SSN in the space provided.

Other corporation. This box is for any corporation other than a personal service corporation. If you check this box, enter the type of corporation (such as insurance company) in the space provided.

Household employer. If you are an individual, check the "Other" box and enter "Household employer" and your SSN. If you are a state or local agency serving as a tax reporting agent for public assistance recipients who become household employers, check the "Other" box and enter "Household employer agent." If you are a trust that qualifies as a household employer, you do not need a separate EIN for reporting tax information relating to household employees; use the EIN of the trust.

QSSS. For a qualified subchapter S subsidiary (QSSS) check the "Other" box and specify "QSSS."

Line 9. Check only **one** box. Do not enter N/A.

Started new business. Check this box if you are starting a new business that requires an EIN. If you check this box, enter the type of business being started. **Do not** apply if you already have an EIN and are only adding another place of business.

Hired employees. Check this box if the existing business is requesting an EIN because it has hired or is hiring employees and is therefore required to file employment tax returns. **Do not** apply if you already have an EIN and are only hiring employees. For information on the applicable employment taxes for family members, see **Circular E**, Employer's Tax Guide (Publication 15).

Created a pension plan. Check this box if you have created a pension plan and need this number for reporting purposes. Also, enter the type of plan created.

Note: *Check this box if you are applying for a trust EIN when a new pension plan is established.*

Banking purpose. Check this box if you are requesting an EIN for banking purposes only, and enter the banking purpose (for example, a bowling league for depositing dues or an investment club for dividend and interest reporting).

Changed type of organization. Check this box if the business is changing its type of organization, for example, if the business was a sole proprietorship and has been incorporated or has become a partnership. If you check this box, specify in the space provided the type of change made, for example, "from sole proprietorship to partnership."

Purchased going business. Check this box if you purchased an existing business. **Do not** use the former owner's EIN. **Do not** apply for a new EIN if you already have one. Use your own EIN.

Created a trust. Check this box if you created a trust, and enter the type of trust created. For example, indicate if the trust is a nonexempt charitable trust or a split-interest trust.

Note: **Do not** *check this box if you are applying for a trust EIN when a new pension plan is established. Check* "Created a pension plan."

Exception. Do **not** file this form for certain grantor-type trusts. The trustee does not need an EIN for the trust if the trustee furnishes the name and TIN of the grantor/owner and the address of the trust to all payors. See the Instructions for Form 1041 for more information.

Other (specify). Check this box if you are requesting an EIN for any reason other than those for which there are checkboxes, and enter the reason.

Line 10. If you are starting a new business, enter the starting date of the business. If the business you acquired is already operating, enter the date you acquired the business. Trusts should enter the date the trust was legally created. Estates should enter the date of death of the decedent whose name appears on line 1 or the date when the estate was legally funded.

Line 11. Enter the last month of your accounting year or tax year. An accounting or tax year is usually 12 consecutive months, either a calendar year or a fiscal year (including a period of 52 or 53 weeks). A calendar year is 12 consecutive months ending on December 31. A fiscal year is either 12 consecutive months ending on the last day of any month other than December or a 52-53 week year. For more information on accounting periods, see **Pub. 538,** Accounting Periods and Methods.

Individuals. Your tax year generally will be a calendar year.

Partnerships. Partnerships generally must adopt one of the following tax years:
- The tax year of the majority of its partners,
- The tax year common to all of its principal partners,
- The tax year that results in the least aggregate deferral of income, or
- In certain cases, some other tax year.

See the **Instructions for Form 1065,** U.S. Partnership Return of Income, for more information.

REMIC. REMICs must have a calendar year as their tax year.

Personal service corporations. A personal service corporation generally must adopt a calendar year unless:
- It can establish a business purpose for having a different tax year, or
- It elects under section 444 to have a tax year other than a calendar year.

Trusts. Generally, a trust must adopt a calendar year except for the following:
- Tax-exempt trusts,
- Charitable trusts, and
- Grantor-owned trusts.

Line 12. If the business has or will have employees, enter the date on which the business began or will begin to pay wages. If the business does not plan to have employees, enter N/A.

Withholding agent. Enter the date you began or will begin to pay income to a nonresident alien. This also applies to individuals who are required to file Form 1042 to report alimony paid to a nonresident alien.

Line 13. For a definition of agricultural labor (farmwork), see **Circular A,** Agricultural Employer's Tax Guide (Publication 51).

Line 14. Generally, enter the exact type of business being operated (for example, advertising agency, farm, food or beverage establishment, labor union, real estate agency, steam laundry, rental of coin-operated vending machine, or investment club). Also state if the business will involve the sale or distribution of alcoholic beverages.

Governmental. Enter the type of organization (state, county, school district, municipality, etc.).

Nonprofit organization (other than governmental). Enter whether organized for religious, educational, or humane purposes, and the principal activity (for example, religious organization—hospital, charitable).

Mining and quarrying. Specify the process and the principal product (for example, mining bituminous coal, contract drilling for oil, or quarrying dimension stone).

Contract construction. Specify whether general contracting or special trade contracting. Also, show the type of work normally performed (for example, general contractor for residential buildings or electrical subcontractor).

Food or beverage establishments. Specify the type of establishment and state whether you employ workers who receive tips (for example, lounge—yes).

Trade. Specify the type of sales and the principal line of goods sold (for example, wholesale dairy products, manufacturer's representative for mining machinery, or retail hardware).

Manufacturing. Specify the type of establishment operated (for example, sawmill or vegetable cannery).

Signature. The application must be signed by (a) the individual, if the applicant is an individual, (b) the president, vice president, or other principal officer, if the applicant is a corporation, (c) a responsible and duly authorized member or officer having knowledge of its affairs, if the applicant is a partnership or other unincorporated organization, or (d) the fiduciary, if the applicant is a trust or an estate.

How To Get Forms and Publications

Phone. You can order forms, instructions, and publications by phone. Just call 1-800-TAX-FORM (1-800-829-3676). You should receive your order or notification of its status within 7 to 15 workdays.

Personal computer. With your personal computer and modem, you can get the forms and information you need using:
- IRS's Internet Web Site at **www.irs.ustreas.gov**
- Telnet at **iris.irs.ustreas.gov**
- File Transfer Protocol at **ftp.irs.ustreas.gov**

You can also dial direct (by modem) to the Internal Revenue Information Services (IRIS) at 703-321-8020. IRIS is an on-line information service on FedWorld.

For small businesses, return preparers, or others who may frequently need tax forms or publications, a CD-ROM containing over 2,000 tax products (including many prior year forms) can be purchased from the Government Printing Office.

CD-ROM. To order the CD-ROM call the Superintendent of Documents at 202-512-1800 or connect to **www.access.gpo.gov/su_docs**

Privacy Act and Paperwork Reduction Act Notice. We ask for the information on this form to carry out the Internal Revenue laws of the United States. We need it to comply with section 6109 and the regulations thereunder which generally require the inclusion of an employer identification number (EIN) on certain returns, statements, or other documents filed with the Internal Revenue Service. Information on this form may be used to determine which Federal tax returns you are required to file and to provide you with related forms and publications. We disclose this form to the Social Security Administration for their use in determining compliance with applicable laws. We will be unable to issue an EIN to you unless you provide all of the requested information which applies to your entity.

You are not required to provide the information requested on a form that is subject to the Paperwork Reduction Act unless the form displays a valid OMB control number. Books or records relating to a form or its instructions must be retained as long as their contents may become material in the administration of any Internal Revenue law. Generally, tax returns and return information are confidential, as required by section 6103.

The time needed to complete and file this form will vary depending on individual circumstances. The estimated average time is:

Recordkeeping	7 min.
Learning about the law or the form	19 min.
Preparing the form	45 min.
Copying, assembling, and sending the form to the IRS . .	20 min.

If you have comments concerning the accuracy of these time estimates or suggestions for making this form simpler, we would be happy to hear from you. You can write to the Tax Forms Committee, Western Area Distribution Center, Rancho Cordova, CA 95743-0001. **Do not** send this form to this address. Instead, see **Where To Apply** on page 2.

WAIVER OF NOTICE

OF THE ORGANIZATION MEETING

OF

_____

We, the undersigned incorporators named in the certificate of incorporation of the above-named corporation hereby agree and consent that the organization meeting of the corporation be held on the date and time and place stated below and hereby waive all notice of such meeting and of any adjournment thereof.

Place of meeting: _____

Date of Meeting: _____

Time of meeting: _____

Dated: _____

_____
Incorporator

_____
Incorporator

_____
Incorporator

MINUTES OF THE ORGANIZATIONAL MEETING OF

INCORPORATORS AND DIRECTORS OF

_____

The organization meeting of the above corporation was held on
_____, 200____ at _____
_____ at ____ o'clock __m.

The following persons were present:

_____   _____

_____   _____

_____   _____

The Waiver of notice of this meeting was signed by all directors and incorporators named in the Articles of Incorporation and filed in the minute book.

The meeting was called to order by _____ an Incorporator named in the Articles of Incorporation. _____ was nominated and elected Chairman and acted as such until relieved by the president. _____ was nominated and elected temporary secretary, and acted as such until relieved by the permanent secretary.

A copy of the Articles of Incorporation which was filed with the Secretary of State of the State of _____ on _____, 200____ was examined by the Directors and Incorporators and filed in the minute book.

The election of officers for the coming year was then held and the following were duly nominated and elected by the Board of Directors to be the officers of the corporation, to serve until such time as their successors are elected and qualified:

President: _____
Vice President: _____
Secretary: _____
Treasurer: _____

The proposed Bylaws for the corporation were then presented to the meeting and discussed. Upon motion duly made, seconded and carried, the Bylaws were adopted and added to the minute book.

A corporate seal for the corporation was then presented to the meeting and upon motion duly made, seconded and carried, it was adopted as the seal of the corporation. An impression thereof was then made in the margin of these minutes

(seal)

The necessity of opening a bank account was then discussed and upon motion duly made, seconded and carried, the following resolution was adopted:

RESOLVED that the corporation open bank accounts with _____ _____ and that the officers of the corporation are authorized to take such action as is necessary to open such accounts; that the bank's printed form of resolution is hereby adopted and incorporated into these minutes by reference and shall be placed in the minute book; that any _____ of the following persons shall have signature authority over the account:

_____   _____
_____   _____
_____   _____

Proposed stock certificates and stock transfer ledger were then presented to the meeting and examined. Upon motion duly made, seconded and carried the stock certificates and ledger were adopted as the certificates and transfer book to be used by the corporation. A sample stock certificate marked "VOID" and the stock transfer ledger were then added to the minute book. Upon motion duly made, seconded and carried, it was then resolved that the stock certificates, when issued, would be signed by the President and the Secretary of the corporation.

The tax status of the corporation was then discussed and it was moved, seconded and carried that the stock of the corporation be issued under §1244 of the Internal Revenue Code and that the officers of the corporation take the necessary action to:

1.   Obtain an employer tax number by filing form SS-4,

2.   ❑   Become an S-Corporation for tax purposes,
      ❑   Remain a C-Corporation for tax purposes,

The expenses of organizing the corporation were then discussed and it was moved, seconded and carried that the corporation pay in full from the corporate funds the expenses and reimburse any advances made by the incorporators upon proof of payment.

The Directors named in the Articles of Incorporation then tendered their resignations, effective upon the adjournment of this meeting. Upon motion duly made, seconded and carried, the following named persons were elected as Directors of the corporation, each to hold office until the first annual meeting of shareholders, and until a successor of each shall have been elected and qualified.

_____

_____

_____

There were presented to the corporation, the following offer(s) to purchase shares of capital stock:

FROM	NO. OF SHARES	CONSIDERATION
_____	_____	_____
_____	_____	_____
_____	_____	_____
_____	_____	_____

The offers were discussed and after motion duly made, seconded and carried were approved. It was further resolved that the Board of Directors has determined that the consideration was valued at least equal to the value of the shares to be issued and that upon tender of the consideration, fully paid non-assessable shares of the corporation be issued.

There being no further business before the meeting, on motion duly made, seconded and carried, the meeting adjourned.

DATED: _____

_____

President

_____

Secretary

BYLAWS OF

_____

A _____ CORPORATION

ARTICLE I - OFFICES

The principal office of the Corporation shall be located in the City of _____ and the State of _____. The Corporation may also maintain offices at such other places as the Board of Directors may, from time to time, determine.

ARTICLE II - SHAREHOLDERS

Section 1 - Annual Meetings: The annual meeting of the shareholders of the Corporation shall be held each year on _____ at _____m. at the principal office of the Corporation or at such other places, within or without the State of _____, as the Board may authorize, for the purpose of electing directors, and transacting such other business as may properly come before the meeting.

Section 2 - Special Meetings: Special meetings of the shareholders may be called at any time by the Board, the President, or by the holders of twenty-five percent (25%) of the shares then outstanding and entitled to vote.

Section 3 - Place of Meetings: All meetings of shareholders shall be held at the principal office of the Corporation, or at such other places as the board shall designate in the notice of such meetings.

Section 4 - Notice of Meetings: Written or printed notice stating the place, day, and hour of the meeting and, in the case of a special meeting, the purpose of the meeting, shall be delivered personally or by mail not less than ten days, nor more than sixty days, before the date of the meeting. Notice shall be given to each Member of record entitled to vote at the meeting. If mailed, such notice shall be deemed to have been delivered when deposited in the United States Mail with postage paid and addressed to the Member at his address as it appears on the records of the Corporation.

Section 5 - Waiver of Notice: A written waiver of notice signed by a Member, whether before or after a meeting, shall be equivalent to the giving of such notice. Attendance of a Member at a meeting shall constitute a waiver of notice of such meeting, except when the Member attends for the express purpose of objecting, at the beginning of the meeting, to the transaction of any business because the meeting is not lawfully called or convened.

Section 6 - Quorum: Except as otherwise provided by Statute, or the Articles of Incorporation, at all meetings of shareholders of the Corporation, the presence at the commencement of such meetings in person or by proxy of shareholders of record holding a majority of the total number of shares of the Corporation then issued and outstanding and entitled to vote, but in no event less than one-third of the shares entitled to vote at the meeting, shall constitute a quorum for the transaction of any business. If any shareholder leaves after the commencement of a meeting, this shall have no effect on the existence of a quorum, after a quorum has been established at such meeting.

Despite the absence of a quorum at any annual or special meeting of shareholders, the shareholders, by a majority of the votes cast by the holders of shares entitled to vote thereon, may adjourn the meeting. At any such adjourned meeting at which a quorum is present, any business may be transacted at the meeting as originally called as if a quorum had been present.

Section 7 - Voting: Except as otherwise provided by Statute or by the Articles of Incorporation, any corporate action, other than the election of directors, to be taken by vote of the shareholders, shall be authorized by a majority of votes cast at a meeting of shareholders by the holders of shares entitled to vote thereon.

Except as otherwise provided by Statute or by the Articles of Incorporation, at each meeting of shareholders, each holder of record of stock of the Corporation entitled to vote thereat, shall be entitled to one vote for each share of stock registered in his name on the stock transfer books of the corporation.

Each shareholder entitled to vote may do so by proxy; provided, however, that the instrument authorizing such proxy to act shall have been executed in writing by the shareholder himself. No proxy shall be valid after the expiration of eleven months from the date of its execution, unless the person executing it shall have specified therein, the length of time it is to continue in force. Such instrument shall be exhibited to the Secretary at the meeting and shall be filed with the records of the corporation.

Any resolution in writing, signed by all of the shareholders entitled to vote thereon, shall be and constitute action by such shareholders to the effect therein expressed, with the same force and effect as if the same had been duly passed by unanimous vote at a duly called meeting of shareholders and such resolution so signed shall be inserted in the Minute Book of the Corporation under its proper date.

ARTICLE III - BOARD OF DIRECTORS

Section 1 - Number, Election and Term of Office: The number of the directors of the Corporation shall be (____) This number may be increased or decreased by the amendment of these bylaws by the Board but shall in no case be less than ____ director(s). The members of the Board, who need not be shareholders, shall be elected by a majority of the votes cast at a meeting of shareholders entitled to vote in the election. Each director shall hold office until the annual meeting of the shareholders next succeeding his election, and until his successor is elected and qualified, or until his prior death, resignation or removal.

Section 2 - Vacancies: Any vacancy in the Board shall be filled for the unexpired portion of the term by a majority vote of the remaining directors, though less than a quorum, at any regular meeting or special meeting of the Board called for that purpose. Any such director so elected may be replaced by the shareholders at a regular or special meeting of shareholders.

Section 3 - Duties and Powers: The Board shall be responsible for the control and management of the affairs, property and interests of the Corporation, and may exercise all powers of the Corporation, except as limited by statute.

Section 4 - Annual Meetings: An annual meeting of the Board shall be held immediately following the annual meeting of the shareholders, at the place of such annual meeting of shareholders. The Board from time to time, may provide by resolution for the holding of other meetings of the Board, and may fix the time and place thereof.

Section 5 - Special Meetings: Special meetings of the Board shall be held whenever called by the President or by one of the directors, at such time and place as may be specified in the respective notice or waivers of notice thereof.

Section 6 - Notice and Waiver: Notice of any special meeting shall be given at least five days prior thereto by written notice delivered personally, by mail or by telegram to each Director at his address. If mailed, such notice shall be deemed to be delivered when deposited in the United States Mail with postage prepaid. If notice is given by telegram, such notice shall be deemed to be delivered when the telegram is delivered to the telegraph company.

Any Director may waive notice of any meeting, either before, at, or after such meeting, by signing a waiver of notice. The attendance of a Director at a meeting shall constitute a waiver of notice of such meeting and a waiver of any and all objections to the place of such meeting, or the manner in which it has been called or convened, except when a Director states at the beginning of the meeting any objection to the transaction of business because the meeting is not lawfully called or convened.

Section 7 - Chairman: The Board may, at its discretion, elect a Chairman. At all meetings of the Board, the Chairman of the Board, if any and if present, shall preside. If there is no Chairman, or he is absent, then the President shall preside, and in his absence, a Chairman chosen by the directors shall preside.

Section 8 - Quorum and Adjournments: At all meetings of the Board, the presence of a majority of the entire Board shall be necessary and sufficient to constitute a quorum for the transaction of business, except as otherwise provided by law, by the Articles of Incorporation, or by these bylaws. A majority of the directors present at the time and place of any regular or special meeting, although less than a quorum, may adjourn the same from time to time without notice, until a quorum shall be present.

Section 9 - Board Action: At all meetings of the Board, each director present shall have one vote, irrespective of the number of shares of stock, if any, which he may hold. Except as otherwise provided by Statute, the action of a majority of the directors present at any meeting at which a quorum is present shall be the act of the Board. Any action authorized, in writing, by all of the Directors entitled to vote thereon and filed with the minutes of the Corporation shall be the act of the Board with the same force and effect as if the same had been passed by unanimous vote at a duly called meeting of the Board. Any action taken by the Board may be taken without a meeting if agreed to in writing by all members before or after the action is taken and if a record of such action is filed in the minute book.

Section 10 - Telephone Meetings: Directors may participate in meetings of the Board through use of a telephone if such can be arranged so that all Board members can hear all other members. The use of a telephone for participation shall constitute presence in person.

Section 11 - Resignation and Removal: Any director may resign at any time by giving written notice to another Board member, the President or the Secretary of the Corporation. Unless otherwise specified in such written notice, such resignation shall take effect upon receipt thereof by the Board or by such officer, and the acceptance of such resignation shall not be necessary to make it effective. Any director may be removed with or without cause at any time by the affirmative vote of shareholders holding of record in the aggregate at least a majority of the outstanding shares of the Corporation at a special meeting of the shareholders called for that purpose, and may be removed for cause by action of the Board.

Section 12 - Compensation: No stated salary shall be paid to directors, as such for their services, but by resolution of the Board a fixed sum and/or expenses of attendance, if any, may be allowed for attendance at each regular or special meeting of the Board. Nothing herein contained shall be construed to preclude any director from serving the Corporation in any other capacity and receiving compensation therefor.

ARTICLE IV - OFFICERS

Section 1 - Number, Qualification, Election and Term: The officers of the Corporation shall consist of a President, a Secretary, a Treasurer, and such other officers, as the Board may from time to time deem advisable. Any officer may be, but is not required to be, a director of the Corporation. The officers of the Corporation shall be elected by the Board at the regular annual meeting of the Board. Each officer shall hold office until the annual meeting of the Board next succeeding his election, and until his successor shall have been elected and qualified, or until his death, resignation or removal.

Section 2 - Resignation and Removal: Any officer may resign at any time by giving written notice of such resignation to the President or the Secretary of the Corporation or to a member of the Board. Unless otherwise specified in such written notice, such resignation shall take effect upon receipt thereof by the Board member or by such officer, and the acceptance of such resignation shall not be necessary to make it effective. Any officer may be removed, either with or without cause, and a successor elected by a majority vote of the Board at any time.

Section 3 - Vacancies: A vacancy in any office may at any time be filled for the unexpired portion of the term by a majority vote of the Board.

<u>Section 4 - Duties of Officers</u>: Officers of the Corporation shall, unless otherwise provided by the Board, each have such powers and duties as generally pertain to their respective offices as well as such powers and duties as may from time to time be specifically decided by the Board. The President shall be the chief executive officer of the Corporation.

<u>Section 5 - Compensation</u>: The officers of the Corporation shall be entitled to such compensation as the Board shall from time to time determine.

<u>Section 6 - Delegation of Duties:</u> In the absence or disability of any Officer of the Corporation or for any other reason deemed sufficient by the Board of Directors, the Board may delegate his powers or duties to any other Officer or to any other Director.

<u>Section 7 - Shares of Other Corporations</u>: Whenever the Corporation is the holder of shares of any other Corporation, any right or power of the Corporation as such shareholder (including the attendance, acting and voting at shareholders' meetings and execution of waivers, consents, proxies or other instruments) may be exercised on behalf of the Corporation by the President, any Vice President, or such other person as the Board may authorize.

ARTICLE V - COMMITTEES

The Board of Directors may, by resolution, designate an Executive Committee and one or more other committees. Such committees shall have such functions and may exercise such power of the Board of Directors as can be lawfully delegated, and to the extent provided in the resolution or resolutions creating such committee or committees. Meetings of committees may be held without notice at such time and at such place as shall from time to time be determined by the committees. The committees of the corporation shall keep regular minutes of their proceedings, and report these minutes to the Board of Directors when required.

ARTICLE VI - BOOKS, RECORDS AND REPORTS

<u>Section 1 - Annual Report:</u> The Corporation shall send an annual report to the Members of the Corporation not later than _____ months after the close of each fiscal year of the Corporation. Such report shall include a balance sheet as of the close of the fiscal year of the Corporation and a revenue and disbursement statement for the year ending on such closing date. Such financial statements shall be prepared from and in accordance with the books of the Corporation, and in conformity with generally accepted accounting principles applied on a consistent basis.

<u>Section 2 - Permanent Records:</u> The corporation shall keep current and correct records of the accounts, minutes of the meetings and proceedings and membership records of the corporation. Such records shall be kept at the registered office or the principal place of business of the corporation. Any such records shall be in written form or in a form capable of being converted into written form.

<u>Section 3 - Inspection of Corporate Records:</u> Any person who is a Voting Member of the Corporation shall have the right at any reasonable time, and on written demand stating the purpose thereof, to examine and make copies from the relevant books and records of accounts, minutes, and records of the Corporation. Upon the written request of any Voting Member, the Corporation shall mail to such Member a copy of the most recent balance sheet and revenue and disbursement statement.

ARTICLE VII- SHARES OF STOCK

<u>Section 1 - Certificates</u>: Each shareholder of the corporation shall be entitled to have a certificate representing all shares which he or she owns. The form of such certificate shall be adopted by a majority vote of the Board of Directors and shall be signed by the President and Secretary of the Corporation and sealed with the seal of the

corporation. No certificate representing shares shall be issued until the full amount of consideration therefore has been paid.

Section 2 - Stock Ledger: The corporation shall maintain a ledger of the stock records of the Corporation. Transfers of shares of the Corporation shall be made on the stock ledger of the Corporation only at the direction of the holder of record upon surrender of the outstanding certificate(s). The Corporation shall be entitled to treat the holder of record of any share or shares as the absolute owner thereof for all purposes and, accordingly, shall not be bound to recognize any legal, equitable or other claim to, or interest in, such share or shares on the part of any other person, whether or not it shall have express or other notice thereof, except as otherwise expressly provided by law.

ARTICLE VIII - DIVIDENDS

Upon approval by the Board of Directors the corporation may pay dividends on its shares in the form of cash, property or additional shares at any time that the corporation is solvent and if such dividends would not render the corporation insolvent.

ARTICLE IX - FISCAL YEAR

The fiscal year of the Corporation shall be the period selected by the Board of Directors as the tax year of the Corporation for federal income tax purposes.

ARTICLE X - CORPORATE SEAL

The Board of Directors may adopt, use and modify a corporate seal. Failure to affix the seal to corporate documents shall not affect the validity of such document.

ARTICLE XI - AMENDMENTS

The Articles of Incorporation may be amended by the Shareholders as provided by _____ statutes. These Bylaws may be altered, amended, or replaced by the Board of Directors; provided, however, that any Bylaws or amendments thereto as adopted by the Board of Directors may be altered, amended, or repealed by vote of the Shareholders. Bylaws adopted by the Members may not be amended or repealed by the Board.

ARTICLE XII - INDEMNIFICATION

Any officer, director or employee of the Corporation shall be indemnified to the full extent allowed by the laws of the State of _____.

Certified to be the Bylaws of the corporation adopted by the Board of Directors on _____, 19____.

_____
Secretary

Banking Resolution of

_____

The undersigned, being the corporate secretary of the above corporation, hereby certifies that on the _____ day of _____, 200___ the Board of Directors of the corporation adopted the following resolution:

RESOLVED that the corporation open bank accounts with _____ _____ and that the officers of the corporation are authorized to take such action as is necessary to open such accounts; that the bank's printed form of resolution is hereby adopted and incorporated into these minutes by reference and shall be placed in the minute book; that any _____ of the following persons shall have signature authority over the account:

_____   _____

_____   _____

and that said resolution has not been modified or rescinded.

Date: _____

_____
Corporate Secretary

(Seal)

<u>Offer to Purchase Stock</u>

Date: _____

To the Board of Directors of

_____

The undersigned, hereby offers to purchase _____ shares of the _____ stock of your corporation at a total purchase price of _____.

Very truly yours,

_____

- -

Offer to Sell Stock
Pursuant to Sec. 1244 I.R.C.

Date: _____

To: _____

Dear

The corporation hereby offers to sell to you _____ shares of its common stock at a price of $_____ per share. These shares are issued pursuant to Section 1244 of the Internal Revenue Code,

Your signature below shall constitute an acceptance of our offer as of the date it is received by the corporation.

Very truly yours,

_____

By:_____

Accepted:

_____

Resolution
of

_____

a _____ Corporation

    RESOLVED that the corporation shall reimburse the following parties for the organizational expenses of the organizers of this corporation and that the corporation shall amortize these expenses as allowed by IRS regulations.

Name	Expense	Amount
_____	_____	$_____
_____	_____	$_____
_____	_____	$_____
_____	_____	$_____
_____	_____	$_____

Date:_____

_____

_____

_____

_____

_____

Bill of Sale

The undersigned, in consideration of the issuance of _____ shares of common stock of _____, a _____ corporation, hereby grants, bargains, sells, transfers and delivers unto said corporation the following goods and chattels:

To have and to hold the same forever.

And the undersigned, their heirs, successors and administrators, covenant and warrant that they are the lawful owners of the said goods and chattels and that they are free from all encumbrances. That the undersigned have the right to sell this property and that they will warrant and defend the sale of said property against the lawful claims and demands of all persons. IN WITNESS whereof the undersigned have executed this Bill of Sale this _____ day of _____200_____.

_____

_____

_____

Form **2553**
(Rev. July 1999)

Department of the Treasury
Internal Revenue Service

Election by a Small Business Corporation
(Under section 1362 of the Internal Revenue Code)
▶ See Parts II and III on back and the separate instructions.
▶ **The corporation may either send or fax this form to the IRS. See page 1 of the instructions.**

OMB No. 1545-0146

Notes: 1. This election to be an S corporation can be accepted only if all the tests are met under **Who may elect** on page 1 of the instructions; all signatures in Parts I and III are originals (no photocopies); and the exact name and address of the corporation and other required form information are provided.

2. Do not file **Form 1120S**, U.S. Income Tax Return for an S Corporation, for any tax year before the year the election takes effect.

3. If the corporation was in existence before the effective date of this election, see **Taxes an S corporation may owe** on page 1 of the instructions.

Part I — Election Information

Please Type or Print

Name of corporation (see instructions)	**A** Employer identification number
Number, street, and room or suite no. (If a P.O. box, see instructions.)	**B** Date incorporated
City or town, state, and ZIP code	**C** State of incorporation

D Election is to be effective for tax year beginning (month, day, year) . . . . ▶ ____/____/____

E Name and title of officer or legal representative who the IRS may call for more information

F Telephone number of officer or legal representative ( )

G If the corporation changed its name or address after applying for the EIN shown in **A** above, check this box . . . . ▶ ☐

H If this election takes effect for the first tax year the corporation exists, enter month, day, and year of the **earliest** of the following: (1) date the corporation first had shareholders, (2) date the corporation first had assets, or (3) date the corporation began doing business . . . . ▶ ____/____/____

I Selected tax year: Annual return will be filed for tax year ending (month and day) ▶ _____

If the tax year ends on any date other than December 31, except for an automatic 52-53-week tax year ending with reference to the month of December, you **must** complete Part II on the back. If the date you enter is the ending date of an automatic 52-53-week tax year, write "52-53-week year" to the right of the date. See Temporary Regulations section 1.441-2T(e)(3).

J Name and address of each shareholder; shareholder's spouse having a community property interest in the corporation's stock; and each tenant in common, joint tenant, and tenant by the entirety. (A husband and wife (and their estates) are counted as one shareholder in determining the number of shareholders without regard to the manner in which the stock is owned.)	**K** Shareholders' Consent Statement. Under penalties of perjury, we declare that we consent to the election of the above-named corporation to be an S corporation under section 1362(a) and that we have examined this consent statement, including accompanying schedules and statements, and to the best of our knowledge and belief, it is true, correct, and complete. We understand our consent is binding and may not be withdrawn after the corporation has made a valid election. (Shareholders sign and date below.)		**L** Stock owned		**M** Social security number or employer identification number (see instructions)	**N** Shareholder's tax year ends (month and day)
	Signature	Date	Number of shares	Dates acquired		

Under penalties of perjury, I declare that I have examined this election, including accompanying schedules and statements, and to the best of my knowledge and belief, it is true, correct, and complete.

Signature of officer ▶ _____ Title ▶ _____ Date ▶ _____

For Paperwork Reduction Act Notice, see page 2 of the instructions. Cat. No. 18629R Form **2553** (Rev. 7-99)

Part II   **Selection of Fiscal Tax Year** (All corporations using this part must complete item O and item P, Q, or R.)

O   Check the applicable box to indicate whether the corporation is:

1. ☐   A new corporation adopting the tax year entered in item I, Part I.
2. ☐   An existing corporation retaining the tax year entered in item I, Part I.
3. ☐   An existing corporation changing to the tax year entered in item I, Part I.

P   Complete item P if the corporation is using the expeditious approval provisions of Rev. Proc. 87-32, 1987-2 C.B. 396, to request **(1)** a natural business year (as defined in section 4.01(1) of Rev. Proc. 87-32) or **(2)** a year that satisfies the ownership tax year test in section 4.01(2) of Rev. Proc. 87-32. Check the applicable box below to indicate the representation statement the corporation is making as required under section 4 of Rev. Proc. 87-32.

1. Natural Business Year ▶ ☐   I represent that the corporation is retaining or changing to a tax year that coincides with its natural business year as defined in section 4.01(1) of Rev. Proc. 87-32 and as verified by its satisfaction of the requirements of section 4.02(1) of Rev. Proc. 87-32. In addition, if the corporation is changing to a natural business year as defined in section 4.01(1), I further represent that such tax year results in less deferral of income to the owners than the corporation's present tax year. I also represent that the corporation is not described in section 3.01(2) of Rev. Proc. 87-32. (See instructions for additional information that must be attached.)

2. Ownership Tax Year ▶ ☐   I represent that shareholders holding more than half of the shares of the stock (as of the first day of the tax year to which the request relates) of the corporation have the same tax year or are concurrently changing to the tax year that the corporation adopts, retains, or changes to per item I, Part I. I also represent that the corporation is not described in section 3.01(2) of Rev. Proc. 87-32.

Note: *If you do not use Item P and the corporation wants a fiscal tax year, complete either Item Q or R below. Item Q is used to request a fiscal tax year based on a business purpose and to make a back-up section 444 election. Item R is used to make a regular section 444 election.*

Q   Business Purpose—To request a fiscal tax year based on a business purpose, you must check box Q1 and pay a user fee. See instructions for details. You may also check box Q2 and/or box Q3.

1. Check here ▶ ☐   if the fiscal year entered in item I, Part I, is requested under the provisions of section 6.03 of Rev. Proc. 87-32. Attach to Form 2553 a statement showing the business purpose for the requested fiscal year. See instructions for additional information that must be attached.

2. Check here ▶ ☐   to show that the corporation intends to make a back-up section 444 election in the event the corporation's business purpose request is not approved by the IRS. (See instructions for more information.)

3. Check here ▶ ☐   to show that the corporation agrees to adopt or change to a tax year ending December 31 if necessary for the IRS to accept this election for S corporation status in the event (1) the corporation's business purpose request is not approved and the corporation makes a back-up section 444 election, but is ultimately not qualified to make a section 444 election, or (2) the corporation's business purpose request is not approved and the corporation did not make a back-up section 444 election.

R   Section 444 Election—To make a section 444 election, you must check box R1 and you may also check box R2.

1. Check here ▶ ☐   to show the corporation will make, if qualified, a section 444 election to have the fiscal tax year shown in item I, Part I. To make the election, you must complete **Form 8716,** Election To Have a Tax Year Other Than a Required Tax Year, and either attach it to Form 2553 or file it separately.

2. Check here ▶ ☐   to show that the corporation agrees to adopt or change to a tax year ending December 31 if necessary for the IRS to accept this election for S corporation status in the event the corporation is ultimately not qualified to make a section 444 election.

Part III   **Qualified Subchapter S Trust (QSST) Election Under Section 1361(d)(2)***

Income beneficiary's name and address	Social security number
Trust's name and address	Employer identification number

Date on which stock of the corporation was transferred to the trust (month, day, year) . . . . ▶   /   /

In order for the trust named above to be a QSST and thus a qualifying shareholder of the S corporation for which this Form 2553 is filed, I hereby make the election under section 1361(d)(2). Under penalties of perjury, I certify that the trust meets the definitional requirements of section 1361(d)(3) and that all other information provided in Part III is true, correct, and complete.

Signature of income beneficiary or signature and title of legal representative or other qualified person making the election	Date

*Use Part III to make the QSST election only if stock of the corporation has been transferred to the trust on or before the date on which the corporation makes its election to be an S corporation. The QSST election must be made and filed separately if stock of the corporation is transferred to the trust after the date on which the corporation makes the S election.

⊛   Form **2553** (Rev. 7-99)

Resolution
of

_____

a _____ Corporation

RESOLVED that the corporation elects "S-Corporation" status for tax purposes under the Internal Revenue Code and that the officers of the corporation are directed to file IRS Form 2553 and to take any further action necessary for the corporation to qualify for S-corporation status.

Shareholders' Consent

The undersigned shareholders being all of the shareholders of the above corporation, a _____ corporation hereby consent to the election of the corporation to obtain S-corporation status

Name and Address of Shareholder	Shares Owned	Date Acquired
_____	_____	_____
_____	_____	_____
_____	_____	_____

Date:_____

_____

_____

_____

_____

_____

WAIVER OF NOTICE OF THE ANNUAL MEETING OF
THE BOARD OF DIRECTORS OF

_____

The undersigned, being all the Directors of the Corporation, hereby agree and consent that an annual meeting of the Board of Directors of the Corporation be held on the _____ day of _____, 200___ at ___ o'clock __m at _____ _____ and do hereby waive all notice whatsoever of such meeting and of any adjournment or adjournments thereof.

We do further agree and consent that any and all lawful business may be transacted at such meeting or at any adjournment or adjournments thereof as may be deemed advisable by the Directors present. Any business transacted at such meeting or at any adjournment or adjournments thereof shall be as valid and legal as if such meeting or adjourned meeting were held after notice.

Date: _____

_____
Director

_____
Director

_____
Director

_____
Director

MINUTES OF THE ANNUAL MEETING OF
THE BOARD OF DIRECTORS OF

_____

     The annual meeting of the Board of Directors of the Corporation was held on the date and at the time and place set forth in the written waiver of notice signed by the directors, and attached to the minutes of this meeting.

     The following were present, being all the directors of the Corporation:

_____   _____

_____   _____

     The meeting was called to order and it was moved, seconded and unanimously carried that _____ act as Chairman and that _____ act as Secretary.

     The minutes of the last meeting of the Board of Directors which was held on _____, 200___ were read and approved by the Board.

     Upon motion duly made, seconded and carried, the following were elected officers for the following year and until their successors are elected and qualify:

President:
Vice President:
Secretary
Treasurer:

     There being no further business to come before the meeting, upon motion duly made, seconded and unanimously carried, it was adjourned.

_____
Secretary

Directors:

_____

_____

_____

_____

WAIVER OF NOTICE OF THE ANNUAL MEETING OF
THE SHAREHOLDERS OF

_____

The undersigned, being all the shareholders of the Corporation, hereby agree and consent that an annual meeting of the shareholders of the Corporation be held on the _____ day of _____, 200___ at ___ o'clock __m at _____ _____ and do hereby waive all notice whatsoever of such meeting and of any adjournment or adjournments thereof.

We do further agree and consent that any and all lawful business may be transacted at such meeting or at any adjournment or adjournments thereof. Any business transacted at such meeting or at any adjournment or adjournments thereof shall be as valid and legal as if such meeting or adjourned meeting were held after notice.

Date: _____

_____
Shareholder

_____
Shareholder

_____
Shareholder

_____
Shareholder

MINUTES OF THE ANNUAL MEETING OF
SHAREHOLDERS OF

_____

The annual meeting of Shareholders of the Corporation was held on the date and at the time and place set forth in the written waiver of notice signed by the shareholders, and attached to the minutes of this meeting.

There were present the following shareholders:

Shareholder   No. of Shares

_____   _____
_____   _____
_____   _____
_____   _____

The meeting was called to order and it was moved, seconded and unanimously carried that _____ act as Chairman and that _____ act as Secretary.

A roll call was taken and the Chairman noted that all of the outstanding shares of the Corporation were represented in person or by proxy. Any proxies were attached to these minutes.

The minutes of the last meeting of the shareholders which was held on _____, 200___ were read and approved by the shareholders.

Upon motion duly made, seconded and carried, the following were elected directors for the following year:

_____   _____
_____   _____

There being no further business to come before the meeting, upon motion duly made, seconded and unanimously carried, it was adjourned.

_____
Secretary

Shareholders:

_____

_____

_____

_____

WAIVER OF NOTICE OF SPECIAL MEETING OF
THE BOARD OF DIRECTORS OF

_____

The undersigned, being all the Directors of the Corporation, hereby agree and consent that a special meeting of the Board of Directors of the Corporation be held on the ____ day of _____, 200___ at ___ o'clock __m at _____ _____ and do hereby waive all notice whatsoever of such meeting and of any adjournment or adjournments thereof.

The purpose of the meeting is:

We do further agree and consent that any and all lawful business may be transacted at such meeting or at any adjournment or adjournments thereof as may be deemed advisable by the Directors present. Any business transacted at such meeting or at any adjournment or adjournments thereof shall be as valid and legal as if such meeting or adjourned meeting were held after notice.

Date: _____

_____
Director

_____
Director

_____
Director

_____
Director

MINUTES OF SPECIAL MEETING OF
THE BOARD OF DIRECTORS OF

_____

A special meeting of the Board of Directors of the Corporation was held on the date and at the time and place set forth in the written waiver of notice signed by the directors, and attached to the minutes of this meeting.

The following were present, being all the directors of the Corporation:

_____   _____

_____   _____

The meeting was called to order and it was moved, seconded and unanimously carried that _____ act as Chairman and that _____ act as Secretary.

The minutes of the last meeting of the Board of Directors which was held on _____, 200___ were read and approved by the Board.

Upon motion duly made, seconded and carried, the following resolution was adopted:

There being no further business to come before the meeting, upon motion duly made, seconded and unanimously carried, it was adjourned.

_____
Secretary

Directors:

_____

_____

_____

_____

WAIVER OF NOTICE OF SPECIAL MEETING OF
THE SHAREHOLDERS OF

_____

The undersigned, being all the shareholders of the Corporation, hereby agree and consent that a special meeting of the shareholders of the Corporation be held on the _____ day of _____, 200___ at ___ o'clock __m at _____ _____ and do hereby waive all notice whatsoever of such meeting and of any adjournment or adjournments thereof.

The purpose of the meeting is

We do further agree and consent that any and all lawful business may be transacted at such meeting or at any adjournment or adjournments thereof. Any business transacted at such meeting or at any adjournment or adjournments thereof shall be as valid and legal as if such meeting or adjourned meeting were held after notice.

Date: _____

_____
Shareholder

_____
Shareholder

_____
Shareholder

_____
Shareholder

MINUTES OF SPECIAL MEETING OF
SHAREHOLDERS OF

_____

A special meeting of Shareholders of the Corporation was held on the date and at the time and place set forth in the written waiver of notice signed by the shareholders, and attached to the minutes of this meeting.

There were present the following shareholders:

Shareholder	No. of Shares
_____	_____
_____	_____
_____	_____
_____	_____

The meeting was called to order and it was moved, seconded and unanimously carried that _____ act as Chairman and that _____ act as Secretary.

A roll call was taken and the Chairman noted that all of the outstanding shares of the Corporation were represented in person or by proxy. Any proxies were attached to these minutes.

The minutes of the last meeting of the shareholders which was held on _____, 200___ were read and approved by the shareholders.

Upon motion duly made, seconded and carried, the following resolution was adopted:

There being no further business to come before the meeting, upon motion duly made, seconded and unanimously carried, it was adjourned.

_____
Secretary

Shareholders:

_____

_____

_____

_____

Change of Registered Agent and/or Registered Office

1. The name of the corporation is:

2. The street address of the current registered office is:

3. The new address of the registered office is to be:

4. The current registered agent is:

5. The new registered agent is:

6. The street address of the registered office and the street address of the business address of the registered agent are identical.

7. Such change was authorized by resolution duly adopted by the Board of Directors of the corporation or by an officer of the corporation so authorized by the board of directors.

_____
Secretary

Having been named as registered agent and to accept service of process for the above stated corporation at the place designated in this certificate, I hereby accept the appointment as registered agent and agree to act in this capacity. I further agree to comply with the provisions of all statutes relating to the proper and complete performance of my duties, and am familiar with and accept the obligations of my position as registered agent.

_____
Registered Agent

Stock Ledger

Certificates Issued

Cert. No.	No. of Shares	Date of Acquisition	Shareholder Name and Address	From Whom Transferred	Amount Paid

Transfer of Shares

Date of Transfer	To Whom Transferred	Cert. No. Surrendered	No. of Shares Transferred	Cert. No.

Received Cert. No. _____

No. of shares _____

New certificates issued:

Cert. No.   No. of Shares

_____   _____

_____   _____

☐ Transferred from: _____

_____

Date: _____

Original   Original   No. of Shares
Cert. No.   No. Shares   Transferred

_____   _____

☐ Original issue

Documentary stamp tax paid:

$ _____

(Attach stamps to this stub.)

Certificate No. _____

No. of shares _____

Dated _____

Issued to: _____

_____

Received Cert. No. _____

No. of shares _____

New certificates issued:

Cert. No.   No. of Shares

_____   _____

_____   _____

☐ Transferred from: _____

_____

Date: _____

Original   Original   No. of Shares
Cert. No.   No. Shares   Transferred

_____   _____

☐ Original issue

Documentary stamp tax paid:

$ _____

(Attach stamps to this stub.)

Certificate No. _____

No. of shares _____

Dated _____

Issued to: _____

_____

Received Cert. No. _____

No. of shares _____

New certificates issued:

Cert. No.   No. of Shares

_____   _____

_____   _____

☐ Transferred from: _____

_____

Date: _____

Original   Original   No. of Shares
Cert. No.   No. Shares   Transferred

_____   _____

☐ Original issue

Documentary stamp tax paid:

$ _____

(Attach stamps to this stub.)

Certificate No. _____

No. of shares _____

Dated _____

Issued to: _____

_____

Stub 1

Certificate No.____
No. of shares ____
Dated ____
Issued to: ____

☐ Original issue
Documentary stamp tax paid:
$____
(Attach stamps to this stub.)

☐ Transferred from: ____
Date: ____

Original Cert. No.	Original No. Shares	No. of Shares Transferred
____	____	____

Received Cert. No.____
No. of shares ____
New certificates issued:

Cert. No.	No. of Shares
____	____

Stub 2

Certificate No.____
No. of shares ____
Dated ____
Issued to: ____

☐ Original issue
Documentary stamp tax paid:
$____
(Attach stamps to this stub.)

☐ Transferred from: ____
Date: ____

Original Cert. No.	Original No. Shares	No. of Shares Transferred
____	____	____

Received Cert. No.____
No. of shares ____
New certificates issued:

Cert. No.	No. of Shares
____	____

Stub 3

Certificate No.____
No. of shares ____
Dated ____
Issued to: ____

☐ Original issue
Documentary stamp tax paid:
$____
(Attach stamps to this stub.)

☐ Transferred from: ____
Date: ____

Original Cert. No.	Original No. Shares	No. of Shares Transferred
____	____	____

Received Cert. No.____
No. of shares ____
New certificates issued:

Cert. No.	No. of Shares
____	____

Certificate No.

Shares

The shares represented by this certificate have not been registered under state or federal securities laws. Therefore, they may not be transferred until the corporation determines that such transfer will not adversely affect the exemptions relied upon.

Organized under the laws of _____

This certifies that _____

_____ is the holder of record of

_____ shares of _____ stock of

transferable only on the books of the corporation by the holder hereof in person or by attorney upon surrender of this certificate properly endorsed.

In witness whereof, the said corporation has caused this certificate to be signed by its duly authorized officers and its corporate seal to be hereto affixed this _____ day of _____, _____.

_____

_____

For value received, _____ *hereby sell, assign and transfer unto* _____

_____,

_____ *shares*

represented by this certificate and do hereby irrevocably constitute and appoint

_____ *attorney to transfer the said shares on*

the books of the corporation with full power of substitution in the premises.

Dated _____

_____

Witness:

_____

Certificate No.

Shares

The shares represented by this certificate have not been registered under state or federal securities laws. Therefore, they may not be transferred until the corporation determines that such transfer will not adversely affect the exemptions relied upon.

Organized under the laws of _____

This certifies that _____ *is the holder of record of* _____ *shares of* _____ *stock of*

transferable only on the books of the corporation by the holder hereof in person or by attorney upon surrender of this certificate properly endorsed.

In witness whereof, the said corporation has caused this certificate to be signed by its duly authorized officers and its corporate seal to be hereto affixed this _____ *day of* _____, _____ .

For value received, _____ hereby sell, assign and transfer unto _____

_____,

_____ shares

represented by this certificate and do hereby irrevocably constitute and appoint

_____ attorney to transfer the said shares on

the books of the corporation with full power of substitution in the premises.

Dated _____

_____

Witness:

_____

The shares represented by this certificate have not been registered under state or federal securities laws. Therefore, they may not be transferred until the corporation determines that such transfer will not adversely affect the exemptions relied upon.

Certificate No.

Shares

Organized under the laws of

This certifies that

is the holder of record of

shares of

stock of

transferable only on the books of the corporation by the holder hereof in person or by attorney upon surrender of this certificate properly endorsed.

In witness whereof, the said corporation has caused this certificate to be signed by its duly authorized officers and its corporate seal to be hereto affixed this _____ day of _____, _____.

For value received, ____ hereby sell, assign and transfer unto _____ shares represented by this certificate and do hereby irrevocably constitute and appoint _____ attorney to transfer the said shares on the books of the corporation with full power of substitution in the premises.

Dated _____

_____

Witness:

_____

Certificate No.

Shares

The shares represented by this certificate have not been registered under state or federal securities laws. Therefore, they may not be transferred until the corporation determines that such transfer will not adversely affect the exemptions relied upon.

Organized under the laws of

This certifies that

is the holder of record of

shares of

stock of

transferable only on the books of the corporation by the holder hereof in person or by attorney upon surrender of this certificate properly endorsed.

In witness whereof, the said corporation has caused this certificate to be signed by its duly authorized officers and its corporate seal to be hereto affixed this ____ day of _____.

For value received, _____ hereby sell, assign and transfer unto _____

_____,

_____ shares

represented by this certificate and do hereby irrevocably constitute and appoint

_____ attorney to transfer the said shares on

the books of the corporation with full power of substitution in the premises.

Dated _____

_____

Witness:

_____

The shares represented by this certificate have not been registered under state or federal securities laws. Therefore, they may not be transferred until the corporation determines that such transfer will not adversely affect the exemptions relied upon.

Certificate No.

Shares

Organized under the laws of

This certifies that _____ *is the holder of record of*

_____ *shares of* _____ *stock of*

transferable only on the books of the corporation by the holder hereof in person or by attorney upon surrender of this certificate properly endorsed.

In witness whereof, the said corporation has caused this certificate to be signed by its duly authorized officers and its corporate seal to be hereto affixed this _____ day of _____, _____.

For value received, _____ hereby sell, assign and transfer unto _____

_____,

_____ shares

represented   by   this   certificate   and   do   hereby   irrevocably   constitute   and   appoint

_____ attorney to transfer the said shares on

the books of the corporation with full power of substitution in the premises.

Dated _____

_____

Witness:

_____

192

INDEX

Your #1 Source for Real World Legal Information...

LEGAL SURVIVAL GUIDES™

• Written by lawyers
• Simple English explanation of the law
• Forms and instructions included

  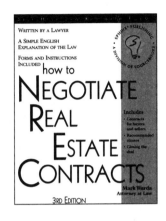

HOW TO REGISTER YOUR OWN COPYRIGHT (3RD EDITION)

All of the information and forms needed to copyright any type of creative work, or how to use the works of others, is contained in this book. Learn to protect written, musical, audiovisual, and three dimensional works, as well as computer programs and designs.

160 pages; $21.95;
ISBN 1-57248-124-2

HOW TO REGISTER YOUR OWN TRADEMARK (3RD EDITION)

This complete guide to protecting a trademark explains state and federal registration, including choosing and searching the mark, preparing and drawing the application, using and protecting the mark, and a registration flow chart to explain the steps.

160 pages; $21.95;
ISBN 1-57248-104-8

HOW TO NEGOTIATE REAL ESTATE CONTRACTS (3RD EDITION)

Buying or selling real estate will be easier with this book, which explains each type of clause found in both residential and commercial real estate contracts, and includes five different contracts for various situations.

128 pages; $18.95;
ISBN 1-57071-332-4

What our customers say about our books:

"It couldn't be more clear for the lay person." —R.D.

"I want you to know I really appreciate your book. It has saved me a lot of time and money." —L.T.

"Your real estate contracts book has saved me nearly $12,000.00 in closing costs over the past year." —A.B.

"...many of the legal questions that I have had over the years were answered clearly and concisely through your plain English interpretation of the law." —C.E.H.

"If there weren't people out there like you I'd be lost. You have the best books of this type out there." —S.B.

"...your forms and directions are easy to follow." —C.V.M.

Legal Survival Guides are directly available from the publisher, or from your local bookstores.
For credit card orders call 1–800–43–BRIGHT, write P.O. Box 4410, Naperville, IL 60567-4410,
or fax 630-961-2168

SPHINX® PUBLISHING'S NATIONAL TITLES
Valid in All 50 States

LEGAL SURVIVAL IN BUSINESS

How to Form a Limited Liability Company	$19.95
How to Form Your Own Corporation (3E)	$19.95
How to Form Your Own Partnership	$19.95
How to Register Your Own Copyright (3E)	$19.95
How to Register Your Own Trademark (3E)	$19.95
Most Valuable Business Legal Forms You'll Ever Need (2E)	$19.95
Most Valuable Corporate Forms You'll Ever Need (2E)	$24.95
Software Law (with diskette)	$29.95

LEGAL SURVIVAL IN COURT

Crime Victim's Guide to Justice	$19.95
Debtors' Rights (3E)	$12.95
Grandparents' Rights (2E)	$19.95
Help Your Lawyer Win Your Case (2E)	$12.95
Jurors' Rights (2E)	$9.95
Legal Research Made Easy (2E)	$14.95
Winning Your Personal Injury Claim	$19.95

LEGAL SURVIVAL IN REAL ESTATE

How to Buy a Condominium or Townhome	$16.95
How to Negotiate Real Estate Contracts (3E)	$16.95
How to Negotiate Real Estate Leases (3E)	$16.95

LEGAL SURVIVAL IN PERSONAL AFFAIRS

Guia de Inmigracion a Estados Unidos (2E)	$19.95
How to File Your Own Bankruptcy (4E)	$19.95
How to File Your Own Divorce (4E)	$19.95
How to Make Your Own Will (2E)	$12.95
How to Write Your Own Living Will (2E)	$12.95
How to Write Your Own Premarital Agreement (2E)	$19.95
How to Win Your Unemployment Compensation Claim	$19.95
Living Trusts and Simple Ways to Avoid Probate (2E)	$19.95
Most Valuable Personal Legal Forms You Will Ever Need	$19.95
Neighbor v. Neighbor (2E)	$12.95
The Nanny and Domestic Help Legal Kit	$19.95
The Power of Attorney Handbook (3E)	$19.95
Quick Divorce Book	$19.95
Social Security Benefits Handbook (2E)	$14.95
Unmarried Parents' Rights	$19.95
U.S.A. Immigration Guide (3E)	$19.95
Your Right to Child Custody, Visitation and Support	$19.95

Legal Survival Guides are directly available from Sourcebooks, Inc., or from your local bookstores.
Prices are subject to change without notice.

For credit card orders call 1–800–43–BRIGHT, write P.O. Box 4410, Naperville, IL 60567-4410
or fax 630-961-2168

SPHINX® PUBLISHING ORDER FORM

BILL TO:	SHIP TO:

Phone #	Terms	F.O.B. Chicago, IL	Ship Date

Charge my: ☐ VISA ☐ MasterCard ☐ American Express

☐ **Money Order or Personal Check**

Credit Card Number

Expiration Date

Qty	ISBN	Title	Retail	Ext.
		SPHINX PUBLISHING NATIONAL TITLES		
	1-57071-166-6	Crime Victim's Guide to Justice	$19.95	
	1-57071-342-1	Debtors' Rights (3E)	$12.95	
	1-57248-082-3	Grandparents' Rights (2E)	$19.95	
	1-57248-087-4	Guia de Inmigracion a Estados Unidos (2E)	$19.95	
	1-57248-103-X	Help Your Lawyer Win Your Case (2E)	$12.95	
	1-57071-164-X	How to Buy a Condominium or Townhome	$16.95	
	1-57071-223-9	How to File Your Own Bankruptcy (4E)	$19.95	
	1-57248-132-3	How to File Your Own Divorce (4E)	$19.95	
	1-57248-100-5	How to Form a DE Corporation from Any State	$19.95	
	1-57248-083-1	How to Form a Limited Liability Company	$19.95	
	1-57248-101-3	How to Form a NV Corporation from Any State	$19.95	
	1-57248-099-8	How to Form a Nonprofit Corporation	$24.95	
	1-57248-133-1	How to Form Your Own Corporation (3E)	$19.95	
	1-57071-343-X	How to Form Your Own Partnership	$19.95	
	1-57248-119-6	How to Make Your Own Will (2E)	$12.95	
	1-57071-331-6	How to Negotiate Real Estate Contracts (3E)	$16.95	
	1-57071-332-4	How to Negotiate Real Estate Leases (3E)	$16.95	
	1-57248-124-2	How to Register Your Own Copyright (3E)	$19.95	
	1-57248-104-8	How to Register Your Own Trademark (3E)	$19.95	
	1-57071-349-9	How to Win Your Unemployment Compensation Claim	$19.95	
	1-57248-118-8	How to Write Your Own Living Will (2E)	$12.95	
	1-57071-344-8	How to Write Your Own Premarital Agreement (2E)	$19.95	
	1-57071-333-2	Jurors' Rights (2E)	$9.95	
	1-57071-400-2	Legal Research Made Easy (2E)	$14.95	
	1-57071-336-7	Living Trusts and Simple Ways to Avoid Probate (2E)	$19.95	
	1-57071-345-6	Most Valuable Bus. Legal Forms You'll Ever Need (2E)	$19.95	

Qty	ISBN	Title	Retail	Ext.
	1-57071-346-4	Most Valuable Corporate Forms You'll Ever Need (2E)	$24.95	
	1-57248-130-7	Most Valuable Personal Legal Forms You'll Ever Need	$19.95	
	1-57248-098-X	The Nanny and Domestic Help Legal Kit	$19.95	
	1-57248-089-0	Neighbor v. Neighbor (2E)	$14.95	
	1-57071-348-0	The Power of Attorney Handbook (3E)	$19.95	
	1-57248-131-5	Quick Divorce Boook	$19.95	
	1-57071-337-5	Social Security Benefits Handbook (2E)	$14.95	
	1-57071-163-1	Software Law (w/diskette)	$29.95	
	1-57071-399-5	Unmarried Parents' Rights	$19.95	
	1-57071-354-5	U.S.A. Immigration Guide (3E)	$19.95	
	1-57071-165-8	Winning Your Personal Injury Claim	$19.95	
	1-57248-097-1	Your Right to Child Custody, Visitation and Support	$19.95	
		CALIFORNIA TITLES		
	1-57071-360-X	CA Power of Attorney Handbook	$12.95	
	1-57248-126-9	How to File for Divorce in CA (2E)	$19.95	
	1-57071-356-1	How to Make a CA Will	$12.95	
	1-57071-358-8	How to Win in Small Claims Court in CA	$14.95	
	1-57071-359-6	Landlords' Rights and Duties in CA	$19.95	
		FLORIDA TITLES		
	1-57071-363-4	Florida Power of Attorney Handbook (2E)	$12.95	
	1-57248-093-9	How to File for Divorce in FL (6E)	$24.95	
	1-57071-380-4	How to Form a Corporation in FL (4E)	$19.95	
	1-57248-086-6	How to Form a Limited Liability Co. in FL	$19.95	
	1-57071-401-0	How to Form a Partnership in FL	$19.95	
	1-57248-113-7	How to Make a FL Will (6E)	$12.95	
	1-57248-088-2	How to Modify Your FL Divorce Judgment (4E)	$22.95	
	Form Continued on Following Page		**SUBTOTAL**	

To order, call Sourcebooks at 1-800-43-BRIGHT or FAX (630)961-2168 (Bookstores, libraries, wholesalers—please call for discount)

Prices are subject to change without notice.

SPHINX® PUBLISHING ORDER FORM

Qty	ISBN	Title	Retail	Ext.
	1-57248-081-5	How to Start a Business in FL (5E)	$16.95	
	1-57071-362-6	How to Win in Small Claims Court in FL (6E)	$14.95	
	1-57248-123-4	Landlords' Rights and Duties in FL (8E)	$19.95	
	GEORGIA TITLES			
	1-57071-376-6	How to File for Divorce in GA (3E)	$19.95	
	1-57248-075-0	How to Make a GA Will (3E)	$12.95	
	1-57248-076-9	How to Start a Business in Georgia	$16.95	
	ILLINOIS TITLES			
	1-57071-405-3	How to File for Divorce in IL (2E)	$19.95	
	1-57071-415-0	How to Make an IL Will (2E)	$12.95	
	1-57071-416-9	How to Start a Business in IL (2E)	$16.95	
	1-57248-078-5	Landlords' Rights & Duties in IL	$19.95	
	MASSACHUSETTS TITLES			
	1-57071-329-4	How to File for Divorce in MA (2E)	$19.95	
	1-57248-115-3	How to Form a Corporation in MA	$19.95	
	1-57248-108-0	How to Make a MA Will (2E)	$12.95	
	1-57248-106-4	How to Start a Business in MA (2E)	$16.95	
	1-57248-107-2	Landlords' Rights and Duties in MA (2E)	$19.95	
	MICHIGAN TITLES			
	1-57071-409-6	How to File for Divorce in MI (2E)	$19.95	
	1-57248-077-7	How to Make a MI Will (2E)	$12.95	
	1-57071-407-X	How to Start a Business in MI (2E)	$16.95	
	NEW YORK TITLES			
	1-57071-184-4	How to File for Divorce in NY	$24.95	
	1-57248-105-6	How to Form a Corporation in NY	$19.95	
	1-57248-095-5	How to Make a NY Will (2E)	$12.95	
	1-57071-185-2	How to Start a Business in NY	$16.95	
	1-57071-187-9	How to Win in Small Claims Court in NY	$14.95	
	1-57071-186-0	Landlords' Rights and Duties in NY	$19.95	

Qty	ISBN	Title	Retail	Ext.
	1-57071-188-7	New York Power of Attorney Handbook	$19.95	
	1-57248-122-6	Tenants' Rights in NY	$19..95	
	NORTH CAROLINA TITLES			
	1-57071-326-X	How to File for Divorce in NC (2E)	$19.95	
	1-57248-129-3	How to Make a NC Will (3E)	$12.95	
	1-57248-096-3	How to Start a Business in NC (2E)	$16.95	
	1-57248-091-2	Landlords' Rights & Duties in NC	$19.95	
	OHIO TITLES			
	1-57248-102-1	How to File for Divorce in OH	$19.95	
	PENNSYLVANIA TITLES			
	1-57248-127-7	How to File for Divorce in PA (2E)	$19.95	
	1-57248-094-7	How to Make a PA Will (2E)	$12.95	
	1-57248-112-9	How to Start a Business in PA (2E)	$16.95	
	1-57071-179-8	Landlords' Rights and Duties in PA	$19.95	
	TEXAS TITLES			
	1-57071-330-8	How to File for Divorce in TX (2E)	$19.95	
	1-57248-114-5	How to Form a Corporation in TX (2E)	$19.95	
	1-57071-417-7	How to Make a TX Will (2E)	$12.95	
	1-57071-418-5	How to Probate an Estate in TX (2E)	$19.95	
	1-57071-365-0	How to Start a Business in TX (2E)	$16.95	
	1-57248-111-0	How to Win in Small Claims Court in TX (2E)	$14.95	
	1-57248-110-2	Landlords' Rights and Duties in TX (2E)	$19.95	

SUBTOTAL THIS PAGE _____

SUBTOTAL PREVIOUS PAGE _____

Illinois residents add 6.75% sales tax

Florida residents add 6% state sales tax plus applicable discretionary surtax _____

Shipping — $4.00 for 1st book, $1.00 each additional _____

TOTAL _____

To order, call Sourcebooks at 1-800-43-BRIGHT or FAX (630)961-2168 (Bookstores, libraries, wholesalers—please call for discount)

Prices are subject to change without notice.